We are a distracted people whose hearts are prone to wander. In *Look, Listen, Live: Cultivating Attention in a Distracting World*, Aimee Joseph gets to the heart of our distractions and helps us attend and focus on the One who never fails to attend to us. This gospel-centered, Christ-exalting, and grace-filled book will help readers practically engage with and be awed by our amazing and wondrous God so we can Look, Listen, and Live.

Christina Fox
Author, *Idols of a Mother's Heart*

*Look, Listen, Live* is not long in length but rich in reflection! Instead of lightly snacking on an appetizer, the reader feasts on the biblical texts, insightful quotes, and personal illustrations woven through each chapter. I recommend this book if you long to be more attuned to the Lord in the busyness and challenges of everyday life.

Paul Kim
Senior Pastor, Redeemer Presbyterian Church, San Diego, California
Author, *Daniel: Standing Firm in Adversity*

Distraction and inattention hound us every day and hinder us from noticing and meditating on truth, goodness, and beauty--the very things that point us to God. That's why I'm so thankful for this book. Aimee Joseph exhorts us with love and wisdom to stop and pay attention to what truly matters and, even better, she tells us how.

Christine Hoover
Author, *More Than Enough: God's Strength in Our Weakness in 2 Corinthians*

*Look, Listen, Live* was just what I needed! It opened my eyes to how often I rush past what matters—reminding me to slow down, be present, and fix my eyes on the Lord. In a world of constant distractions, this book will help you stay awake to beauty, anchored in presence, and attentive to God's grace in suffering.

Vaneetha Risner
Author, *Watching for the Morning*


Don't let the title fool you. *Look, Listen, Live* is more than a call to pay attention. It's an invitation to cultivating deeper affection and adoration for Christ. In an increasingly distracted, disengaged, and noisy world, Aimee Joseph offers a wise and winsome guide to recovering attentiveness to what matters most in life: the beauty and worth of the Living God.

Beverly Berrus
Bible teacher and author


In an age of death scroll distractions, never has the adage, we become what we behold been more relevant. Aimee's gentle yet compelling style invites readers to look up and listen intently so we might be captivated by the beauty and blessing of a life devoted to the worship of God Almighty. Seeing really does lead to believing!

Karen Hodge
Coordinator of Women's Ministries, Presbyterian Church in America;
author, *Transformed: Life-taker to Life-giver*

AIMEE JOSEPH

# LOOK
# LISTEN
# LIVE

## CULTIVATING ATTENTION IN A DISTRACTED CULTURE

CHRISTIAN
FOCUS

Scripture quotations are from The Holy Bible, English Standard Version, copyright © 2001 by Crossway Bibles, a publishing ministry of Good News Publishers. Used by permission. All rights reserved. esv Text Edition: 2011.

Scripture quotations marked (NIV) are taken from the HOLY BIBLE, NEW INTERNATIONAL VERSION®. NIV®. Copyright©1973, 1978, 1984 by International Bible Society. Used by permission of Zondervan. All rights reserved.

Copyright © Aimee Joseph 2025

paperback ISBN 978-1-5271-1273-5
ebook ISBN 978-1-5271-1371-8

Published in 2025 by
Christian Focus Publications Ltd,
Geanies House, Fearn, Ross-shire,
IV20 1TW, Great Britain.
www.christianfocus.com

Cover design by Rhian Muir

Printed and bound by Bell and Bain, Glasgow

All rights reserved. No part of this publication may be reproduced, stored in a retrieval system, or transmitted, in any form, by any means, electronic, mechanical, photocopying, recording or otherwise without the prior permission of the publisher or a licence permitting restricted copying. In the U.K. such licences are issued by the Copyright Licensing Agency, 4 Battlebridge Lane, London, SE1 2HX. www.cla.co.uk

To Richard and Laura Sherman,
my parents who taught me to pay attention to beauty

# Contents

| | |
|---|---|
| Acknowledgements | ix |
| Introduction | 1 |

## Part I

| | |
|---|---|
| Chapter 1: Our Attentive God | 9 |
| Chapter 2: Attention Leads to Adoration | 21 |
| Chapter 3: Inattention and Alloyed Attention | 37 |
| Chapter 4: Faith and Focus | 53 |

## Part II

| | |
|---|---|
| Chapter 5: The Pathway of Presence | 71 |
| Chapter 6: The Pathway of Beauty | 87 |
| Chapter 7: The Pathway of Pain | 103 |
| Conclusion | 119 |

# Acknowledgements

I know that every writing project requires a village, but I have felt it more in the writing of this book than in any other. Without the thoughtful leadership of Randy and Clara Maranville and Sami Shaker, I would still be standing at the trailhead of the path that leads to cultivated attention. By God's grace and through the companionship of an incredible cohort of women, I am a bit further down the path of an attentive life. Shelley, Wendy, Safi, Aisha, Liz, Jennifer, Robin, Joy, Dottie, Chelsea, and Dana, my time with you shaped my soul deeply. Thanks for your careful attention to God and to others. Thank you to the team at Christian Focus on the other side of the pond for taking on this project. My husband, G'Joe, and our three boys, Tyus, Eli, and Phin, deserve the lion's share of gratitude and acknowledgement. They have taught me more about the attentiveness of God than any book ever could. For from Him and to Him and through Him are all things. To Him be glory forever (Rom. 11:36).

# Introduction

I grew up in a household with a phone attached to the wall. My mother had an unthinkably long cord that would allow her to chat on the phone with her best friend while reaching from our harvest gold-colored kitchen to the laundry room on the other side of the house. I thought she was the queen of multi-tasking as she helped us with math homework, attempted to cook dinner, and folded laundry seemingly simultaneously. As complicated as her feat appeared to me at the time, compared to the lives we now lead on the other side of digital devices, those days seemed simple and focused.

According to an article from Business Insider, the average person touches his or her cell phone 2,617 times a day.[1] This means that thousands of times a day we shift our focus from what we are doing to check our phones willingly, albeit often unconsciously and habitually. That's not to mention the average of forty-six push notifications from apps that interrupt us and steal our attention.[2]

## The Dawn of Distraction

It's not that distraction dawned with the age of the smartphone; the human heart was prone to distraction long before the

---

1. https://pages.dscout.com/hubfs/downloads/dscout_mobile_touches_study_2016.pdf?_ga=2.180416224.67221035.1650551540-199217915.1650551540

2. https://www.businessofapps.com/marketplace/push-notifications/research/push-notifications-statistics/

technological age (or the agricultural age or the Iron Age). However, the modern world has exacerbated and exaggerated our tendency towards distraction. Even before the age of the cell phone and the internet, back when my mom was getting tangled up in her twenty-foot phone cord, social critic Neil Postman noted a strong tendency toward distraction and inattention in the American public. He compared the diminishing attention span and life of the mind of the average American to the days when the general American public was happily willing to sit for seven hours to listen to a series of debates between Abraham Lincoln and Stephen A. Douglas.[3] Today, our presidential debates last a few hours, and most people merely watch the highlight reel on social media feeds for thirty seconds.

To be clear, since the fateful meeting of Adam and Eve with the Serpent in the Garden of Eden, there has been a war for our attention and affection. The world, the flesh, and the enemy of God have been honing their distraction skills for thousands of years; however, the war for our attention entered a new era with recent technological advancements. Just as the machine gun and the U-boat transformed modern warfare, the battle for our attention has ratcheted up a notch with the age of the smartphone. Companies spend millions of dollars researching how to keep our eyes and minds tethered to a screen or an app. Apparently our attention is worth millions to the consumer market. Thankfully, it is worth far more to our God.

## The Art of Attention

Our distractibility has even deeper, more lasting ramifications when it comes to relationships. When we first became parents, our dear friends who were a few years ahead of us told a convicting story about how their toddler taught them just how distractable they were, even as intentional, engaged

---

3. Postman, Neil. *Amusing Ourselves to Death: Public Discourse in the Age of Show Business.* (New York: Penguin Books, 1985), 44.

parents. The father would come home from work during his lunch break (I told you they were thoughtful, present parents) to spend time with his toddler daughter and son. Toddlers tend to have a lot to say, so the dad would sometimes slip into the pattern of shaking his head and saying, "Mmm hmm, mmm hmm," thinking he could pull the wool over her eyes. The two-year-old daughter caught on to the ruse and started grabbing his chin during the conversations, chiding him, "No say 'Mmm hmmm'." It seems that even a toddler understands that attention is a sign of affection. As silly and innocent as the story sounds, we use that line often in our household to gently point out distraction and ask for focused attention from each other: "No say, 'Mmm hmm'" has become code in our home for "Please give me your undivided attention."

We live in a distracting world and distracted souls live within us. In such a world, the art of attention and noticing must be carefully cultivated. If this is true of ordinary subjects like learning calculus or how to knit or conversations with a toddler, how much more should it be true when it comes to the most complex and most satisfying subject of our attention: the God of the universe who desires a focused relationship with each of us. J.I. Packer wisely notes, "The more complex the object, the more complex is the knowing of it."[4] If it takes hundreds of hours of focused attention to learn a second language and scores of hours to acquire rudimentary skill on an instrument, how much more focused attention and intentionality must it take to grow in knowledge of, and appreciation for, an infinitely inexhaustible God?

## Worthy of Wonder

The God who created all things, and still sustains all things with His Word, commands our attention to Him and His Word (Gen. 1; Exod. 20:1-6; Deut. 8:11; Heb. 1:1-3). Underneath the command to acknowledge Him and remember Him as

---

4. Packer, J.I. *Knowing God*. (Downers Grove: Intervarsity Press, 1972), 30.

Lord, GOD is inviting us to do the very thing for which we were created, and which tends toward our thriving. As the Westminster Shorter Catechism reminds us in its first question and answer, "What is the chief end [purpose] of man? Man's chief end is to glorify God and enjoy him forever."[5]

The God who made the wonders of this world is worthy of our wonder (Ps. 19:1-6). The God who gave us His Word is worthy of our attention and obedience to it (Ps. 19:7-14). The God who wired our brains for complex thinking and focused interaction is worthy of the work it takes to think of Him and fight to be present with Him (Pss. 8:3-6, 139:13-14). As C.H. Spurgeon wisely notes, "The highest science, the loftiest speculation, the mightiest philosophy, which can ever engage the attention of a child of God, is the name, the nature, the person, the work, the doings, and the existence of the great God whom he calls his Father."[6]

## Prone To Wander

If you are like me, you agree wholeheartedly with these statements, and upon hearing them, you are like the Ancient Israelites whose immediate response to hearing God's laws given by Moses was a hearty, "All that the LORD has spoken we will do" (Exod. 19:8). But our similarity to the Israelites goes beyond their vow and bleeds into their near-immediate failure to follow through with it. I know the Lord is worthy of my wonder and rightly deserves my attention, but even as I agree, my heart devolves into distractions and my soul stares at lesser things. The deeply entrenched rut of unrighteousness in the human heart moves us quickly from worshiping and serving the creator to worshiping and serving created things (Rom. 1: 21-23). We are *incurvatus in se* (curved in on ourselves) when we ought to be bent in bowing adoration to God. Long

---

5. Williamson, G.I. *The Westminster Confession of Faith for Study Classes.* (Philadelphia: Presbyterian & Reformed, 1946), 46.

6. Spurgeon, C.H. as quoted in *Knowing God*, 13.

before the Latin term was coined, God called out such idolatry in His people (Isa. 41: 21-29) while simultaneously inviting them back to worship of Him. We hear the longing of His heart for us to acknowledge and adore Him, both for His glory and our good, through the words of the prophet Isaiah:

> Why do you spend your money for that which is not bread, and your labor for that which does not satisfy? Listen diligently to me, and eat what is good, and delight yourselves in rich food. Incline your ear, and come to me, hear, that your soul may live; and I will make with you an everlasting covenant, my steadfast, sure love for David (Isa. 55:2-3).

God calls us out for looking on lesser, lower things while ignoring His glorious invitation to come and be with Him. He uses language from nearly all the senses (tasting, seeing, and hearing), corralling our attention. He bids us look and listen to Him that we might live!

We pray with David, "One thing have I asked of the Lord, that will I seek after: that I may dwell in the house of the Lord all the days of my life, to gaze upon the beauty of the Lord and to inquire in his temple" (Ps. 27:4). Yet, we quickly move from gazing upon the Lord to gazing upon ourselves, our loved ones, our schedules, and our concerns. We slip into glancing at the Lord and gazing upon lesser things when the Lord would have it the other way. He deserves our gaze, while the world and the things of this world need only a glance.

All the while, our gracious God is saying to us, "I will instruct you and teach you in the way you should go; I will counsel you with my eye upon you. Be not like a horse or a mule, without understanding, which must be curbed with bit and bridle, or it will not stay near you" (Ps. 32:8-9). I don't know about you, but I do need some breaking with bit and bridle so that I will learn the art of adoration and the science of staying near to God.

## Postured To Learn

If you find God worthy of wonder yet your heart prone to wander, this book is an invitation to learn the art of cultivating attention in a distracting world. Due to our previously admitted distraction, this book will be divided into two parts, in the hopes that we will better focus! In Part I, we will begin by looking long and lovingly at our attentive God: one who sees, hears, and moves towards His people. We will explore the connection between adoration and attention, as Jesus said, "For where your treasure is, there your heart will be also" (Matt. 6:21). We will do a deep dissection into our divided and distracted hearts, addressing the idolatry and lies that hijack our attention from God. After looking at our inattention, our intermittent attention, and our alloyed attention, we will explore ways to cultivate a focused faith. We will conclude Part I by studying three different forms of curiosity, showing biblical examples of each.

As we move into Part II, we will explore three major pathways of cultivating attention toward God and others: the pathway of presence (being where we are, with whom we are, as we are), the pathway of beauty (nature, poetry, art, and music), and the surprising but proven pathway of suffering. In each of these pathways, we will consider practical ways to practice focused attention. As we learn to look longer and focus the beam of our attention, we will discover growing affection for the God who made us from love for love. As we lift our gaze, by the help of our God, we will discover the God who is there, gazing upon us by His grace!

# Part I

# Chapter One

# Our Attentive God

What we believe about God bleeds into our experiences of Him. If, according to the pervasive modern deistic sentiment, we believe God to be a disinterested watchmaker, we will experience a life distant and detached from His care and concern. If, on the other hand, we believe God to be a divine puppeteer, deciding our lives and moving us around like pawns on a chessboard, we won't give our attention to Him because our attention would not matter anyway. Thankfully, the God of the Scriptures is far from a disengaged creator or a power-hungry puppeteer. From the very first chapter of Genesis to the very last chapter of Revelation, God reveals Himself to us as engaged and attentive, intimately acquainted and involved in creation. Our God is one who sees and hears His people. He is our Triune God who loves us as the engaged Father, the incarnate Son, and the indwelling Holy Spirit.

## Created to be Attentive to God

In the first two chapters of Genesis, we learn about God's good intentions for the world and all therein. We see the entire Trinity at work together in creating everything out of nothing (*ex nihilo*). We hear hints at the inter-Trinitarian conversation that happened before creation (Gen. 1:26-27). We were created out of the perfect relational fullness that existed within the Godhead. God the Father spoke through God the Son as God the Spirit hovered over the deep (Gen. 1:2). In Proverbs, we hear poetic hints of Jesus having been present with God at creation (Prov. 8:22-31). In the New Testament, we learn explicitly that Jesus upholds creation by the power of His Word (Heb. 1:1-3). The entire Trinity is fully engaged in both the original act of creation and the ongoing sustaining of all that God has made – and this includes us!

We were created by a graciously attentive God, but we were also created to give our creator our full and undivided attention. God Himself tells us this explicitly through the prophet Isaiah, "Bring my sons from afar and my daughters from the end of the earth, everyone who is called by my name, whom I created for my glory, whom I formed and made" (Isa. 43:6-7). We were created to give our attention to God and to rightly enjoy all the things that He made. God created an environment for created humanity to live in communion, connection, and purpose with Him. Adoring relationship with Him was to be both the context and the very content of our lives.

Adam and Eve, the two creatures who received God's "very good" (*meod tov*), enjoyed intimate interaction with their creator (Gen. 1:29-31). They were in the habit of walking with God in the garden of His making (Gen. 3:8). Peace abounded as they looked to Him for direction, listened to His loving commands, and prioritized life with Him.

It only took a seed of doubt whispered by God's enemy to draw their attention away from God and unto self. The serpent drew Eve's eyes away from a trusting gaze in her creator, enticing her to stare at the fruit of the forbidden tree (Gen. 3:6). Her physical eyes mirrored the action of her soul, as she was drawn from God to self. The early church father, Athanasius, who lived in A.D. 300 and helped write the Nicene Creed, defines idolatry as a turning of human attention away from God and towards themselves, their concerns, and their immediate surroundings.[1]

Even after their tragic choice to disobey, God pursued His people. Though He knew all that happened, God engaged them through questions (Gen. 3:9, 11, 13). Hereto, Athanasius offers insight into the sense of nakedness Adam and Eve experienced after their fall into sin. He writes, "They knew that they were not so much naked of clothing, but that they had become naked of the contemplation of divine things, and that they had turned their minds in the opposite direction."[2] The very nature of their sin stemmed from their shifting their attention from God to created things. The apostle Paul writes similarly when seeking to define idolatry in the first chapter of Romans:

> For although they knew God, they did not honor him as God or give thanks to him, but they became futile in their thinking, and their foolish hearts were darkened. Claiming to be wise, they became fools, and exchanged the glory of the immortal God for images resembling mortal man and birds and animals and creeping things. (Rom. 1:21-23).

In what is known as the protoevangelion, God slaughters an animal to provide clothing for Adam and Eve who, newly aware of their nakedness before God, were hiding behind fig leaves (Gen. 3:21). This sacrifice and shedding of blood to cover their guilt and shame is the earliest hint of the ultimate, once-for-all sacrifice of Jesus Christ (Heb. 10:4-11).

Though God's very good creation rebelled against Him and transgressed His law, God remained attentive to them. Though their sin defaced and deformed His good creation, God showed mercy. God continues to create ways for them to

---

1. John Behr's Introduction to *On the Incarnation*. Saint Athanasius. (Yonkers: St. Vladimir's Seminary Press, 2011), 28.

2. Ibid

be in mediated communication with Him through covenants He initiated. In His covenant with Noah, He promises to never flood the earth again (Gen. 8:20-22). He continues to engage with, and bless, His belligerent children. In His covenant with Abram, God promises to create a people for Himself through whom He will bless all the nations of the earth (Gen. 12:1-3, 15:1-6). God came to Abram and set His favor upon him and his future family. He promised to engage with them and be attentive towards them, not for anything they had done, but out of His own nature and will (Deut. 7:6-10). The more God engaged with His people, the more we learn of His name, character, and gracious intentions. God slowly revealed more of Himself to His people in the process known as progressive revelation.

## The God who Sees

Though God promised to make Abram a father of many nations, Abram and his wife Sarai had no children. After living ten years in the land of Canaan, barren Sarai became impatient and came up with her own plan to provide children for Abram: he should simply sleep with her Egyptian maid, Hagar. Unfortunately, rather than listen to the Lord with faith, Abram listened to his wife with fear (Gen. 16:2). Hagar becomes pregnant, which, rather than solve her problems, only created more problems. A jealous Sarai acts cruelly and contemptuously to her servant (who sadly had no say in the scheme as a servant); Abram continues his passive pandering to his angry wife; and eventually, a haggard Hagar runs away from the awful situation.

Amid a faithless decision, God shows Himself faithful and reveals Himself as the God who sees. The Angel of the Lord finds her in the wilderness, names her, notes her situation, and graciously engages her (Gen. 16:7-9). Here the attentiveness of God is on display even to one with whom He is not in a covenant relationship. In a culture in which she was a double outcast as both a servant and a woman, God comes to her and communes with her. He acknowledges the awful situation Sarai has sinfully created. He promises her and her son in utero protection and provision even though He was not bound by the covenant to do so (Gen. 16:10-12).

Hagar's response to God gives us one of the most beautiful names of God in the Old Testament: "So she called the name of the LORD who spoke to her, 'You are a God of seeing,' for she said, 'Truly here I have seen him who looks after me'" (Gen. 16:13).

Ours is the God who sees. God saw not only a mistreated Egyptian servant and her child but also a faithless Sarai, whom He still blesses with the promised child. God saw Abram's passivity yet still graciously enabled him to become a patriarch. The pattern of God's wayward children and their attentive, gracious God continues as the story unfolds. Though His people continued to look away from Him, He continued to look after them.

## The God who Hears

If Hagar, the Egyptian slave, taught us about the God who sees, the plight of God's people enslaved in Egypt teaches us about the God who hears. Many generations after Abram and Sarai God continued to fulfill His promise. The line begun through the promised son, Isaac, became a people so numerous that their Egyptian captors felt threatened by their presence (Exod. 1:7-14). As God's people groaned, their God heard.

> During those many days the king of Egypt died, and the people of Israel groaned because of their slavery and cried out for help. Their cry for rescue from slavery came up to God. And God heard their groaning, and God remembered his covenant with Abraham, with Isaac, and with Jacob. God saw the people of Israel—and God knew. (Exod. 2:23-25)

God's hearing and seeing led to the deliverance of His people. When our God sees, He acts. When He hears, He moves. In fact, even before the verses above, God had already set the stage for their soon-to-be-deliverer, Moses. When God encounters the shepherd Moses at a strangely burning bush in Midian, God reiterates His attentive care:

> I have surely seen the affliction of my people who are in Egypt and have heard their cry because of their taskmasters. I know their suffering, and I have come down to deliver them out of the hand of the Egyptians and to bring them up out of that land to a good and broad land (Exod. 3:7-8).

In His first major act of deliverance, God frees His people from enslavement to the Egyptians through Moses as a deliverer (Exod. 4–15). However, this act of physical deliverance points to the ultimate deliverance which would come through Jesus, the better Moses, who would deliver His people from their sin. The same God who saw and heard His people crying out in Egypt, saw and heard His people groaning under their slavery to sin. Though they continued to break His covenants with them, God Himself would come to their rescue, fulfilling both sides of the covenant. Where the first Adam failed to be attentive to God, the second Adam, Christ, gave His full attention to God (Rom. 5:12-21). Where the nation of Israel failed to be attuned to God, Christ, the true Israel, attuned to God perfectly (Deut. 8:1-4; Matt. 4:1-17).

Christ perfectly obeyed God, always listening to the Father and living under His loving gaze (John 12:49-50). Yet, Christ willingly submitted to the cross to bear the penalty we earned for turning our eyes from God and being deaf to His laws (1 Pet. 2:24). On the cross, the Father turned away from Christ and closed His ears to His cries that He might enter back into unhindered relationship with His wayward children (2 Cor. 5:21). Those who confess with their mouth and believe in their heart that Jesus is Lord get to share in God's delight over His son, Jesus (Rom. 10:9). The adoring attention Christ receives from the Father is now theirs as adopted children and fellow heirs with Christ (Rom. 8:15-17).

## He Still Sees and Hears

While many of us assent intellectually to the idea that our God sees and hears us, few of us live in the confidence and assurance afforded to us as sons and daughters of God. To borrow terms from A.W. Tozer, our verbal creed does not match our lived creed. We say with our lips, "Jesus Christ is the same yesterday and today and forever," but we show by our lives that we doubt His attentive care (Heb. 13:8). The same Christ who saw and heard His followers on earth sees and hears His followers today.

Christ's Ascension to the Father means that He is presently both enthroned and engaged. He sits enthroned at the right hand of the throne of God as one who has earned the name above all names (Phil. 2:9-11). Yet, our enthroned King of Kings and Lord of LORDS does not lean back, disinterested and distant from the goings-on of His people on earth. He uses His position to actively pray for us (Heb. 7:25). From the throne, He sees, hears, and intimately knows all as an engaged redeemer. His Ascension also ushered His sending forth of the Holy Spirit, the Third Person of the Trinity. Jesus' homecoming to the Father enabled the sending of the Holy Spirit, an attentive, indwelling advocate for the children of God.

The apostle Peter commands us to cast our cares on the one who cares for us (1 Pet. 4:19). He challenges us to continually entrust ourselves to our faithful creator, even and especially when we are in pain and suffering and He sometimes feels far off (1 Pet. 5:7). In fact, Peter reminds suffering believers that though they cannot see God (or feel Him in their difficult circumstances), God attentively keeps both them and their imperishable, unfading inheritance (1 Pet. 1:3-5). Similarly, the writer of Hebrews reminded the Jewish believers of the attentive, watchful eyes of their God (Heb. 4:13).

The same Jesus who heard the cries of blind Bartimaeus and felt the hemorrhaging woman touch His garment even in the middle of a pressing crowd hears us and feels our burdens (Mark 10:46-52; Luke 8:43-48). The same God who gave focused attention to the isolated Samaritan woman at the well offers His focused attention to His children today (John 4:7-26). He calls us His prized possession and continues to guard us as the apple of His eye (Deut. 14:2, 32:10). He also invites us to become like Him in giving focused attention to those around us (Mark 12:30-31). The way He loves us attentively and sacrificially becomes the new standard by which we are to love one another (John 15:12-17).

When Christ returns, bringing with Him the new heaven and the new earth, we will finally, forever be freed from sinful inattention. We will join the elders and the angels who fall before the throne and before the Lamb, saying, "Blessing and glory and wisdom and thanksgiving and honor and power and might be to our God forever and ever! Amen" (Rev. 7:12).

Until then, our souls need constant attention and shepherding. Like sheep, we are prone to wander from the fold of God (Isa. 53:6; 1 Pet. 2:25). Thankfully, the God who hinted throughout the Old Testament of His role as our soul's shepherd fully revealed Himself as the good shepherd through the person of Christ (Ps. 28:9; John 10:11). The good shepherd was also the perfect Lamb of God led to slaughter to bring us into His fold (Isa. 53:7; John 10:7-18). We learn so much about the attentiveness of our God by diving into the shepherding analogy He gives us.

## The Good Shepherd

Psalm 23 is known, even by those outside the Christian faith, for its beautiful poetry and poignant imagery. Although many are drawn to the opening lines, "The LORD is my shepherd, I shall not want," few have a working knowledge of what shepherding entails (Ps. 23:1).

I live in San Diego, where to own a small backyard of turf is quite an accomplishment. I clearly don't interact with sheep on a regular basis. I did, however, spend a summer in Wales as a high schooler. My time in the Welsh countryside confirmed for me the commonly held notion that sheep are stupid and in desperate need of an attentive shepherd. Recently, I read the story of a modern-day shepherd in the historic Lake District of England. James Rebanks went to Oxford seeking to escape the family business of shepherding; however, after graduating, he chose to return to his familial land and continue in the family business. His honest account of the art of shepherding had me laughing, crying, and tired all at the same time. His description below explains the scores of unseen jobs that shepherds do seasonally to simply keep their sheep alive and well:

> Much of the day-to-day work on a farm is spent on the hundreds of little un-newsworthy jobs that are required in managing the land and sheep. Mending walls. Chopping logs. Treating lame sheep. Worming lambs. Moving sheep between fields. Running sheep through the footbath. Laying hedges...Hanging gates. Cleaning the rainwater gutters on buildings. Dipping sheep. Trimming sheep feet. Rescuing lambs from being stuck in fences. Mucking out the dogs. Trimming the muck from the tails of ewes and lambs. As you drive past, you wouldn't notice them, but they add up over time.[3]

Shepherding is far from a glorious, peaceful calling. It requires an intimate knowledge of each sheep – its personality, tendencies and needs. It requires careful, thoughtful maintenance of the ground on which the flock eats, breeds, and sleeps. Shepherding

---

3. Rebanks, James. *The Shepherd's Life: Modern Dispatches from an Ancient Landscape.* (New York: Flatiron Books, 2015), 55.

does not have on and off hours. It involves proper protection of the sheep, fence-mending, and sleepless nights to protect from predators. In short, shepherds must be among the most attentive people alive.

Thankfully, our God is the inexhaustible, untiring shepherd of His flock. Unlike human shepherds who grow weary and fall asleep on their night watches, our God neither sleeps nor slumbers (Ps. 121:4). He is our constant, all-wise keeper who never fails to protect His sheep (Ps. 121:5-8). In fact, Jesus promises that not one sheep given to Him will be lost (John 17:6-12). He who has already laid down His life for us continues to give Himself to us as our keeper, protector, nurturer, and guide. He tells us, as He told His own flock of disciples, "Do not fear, little flock, it is your Father's good pleasure to give you the kingdom" (Luke 12:32).

## The Tools of a Shepherd

We do get a few things right in the popular images of Christ as the good shepherd. He usually carries a shepherd's crook, a tool modern shepherds still use. In the words of Rebanks, "A crook is as essential now on our farm as it ever was. My crook is an extension of my arm, letting me catch the sheep."[4] A crook is used to pull a fleeing sheep toward the shepherd or to pull up a fallen sheep from a dangerous position or place. Phillip Keller, another shepherd who later became a believer in Christ and shared his rich knowledge of shepherding with the church at large, explains the purpose of the rod and the staff mentioned by David (Ps. 23:4). Regarding the rod, Keller wrote the following:

> The rod was in fact, an extension of the owner's right arm. It stood as a symbol of his strength, his power, his authority in any serious situation. The rod was what he relied on to safeguard both himself and his flock in

---

4. Ibid, 159.

danger. And it was, furthermore, the instrument he used to discipline and correct any wayward sheep that insisted on wandering away.[5]

Our alert, good shepherd likewise uses tools to get our attention and to keep us near Him (which is the safest place for a sheep to be). As His sheep, we are to submit to Him and seek to live our lives under His Word and in His presence. When we go astray, get distracted, or even ensnared, God rightly gets our attention. As the writer of Hebrews understood, "The Lord disciplines the one he loves, and chastises every son whom he receives" (Heb. 12:6). Our shepherd will use circumstances, the body and Word of Christ, and the Holy Spirit to get our attention. Thankfully, we can trust the tools of the shepherd because we know His heart. He only disciplines us for our good and for His glory. The writer of Hebrews continues, "For the moment all discipline seems painful rather than pleasant, but later it yields the peaceful fruit of righteousness to those who have been trained by it" (Heb. 12:11). The shepherd will lead us faithfully through the valley and make us to lie down in green pastures; He will restore our souls (Ps. 23:2-3). We would do well to pay attention to Him who pays such close attention to us.

## Watching the One Who Watches Over Us

Most of our fear and anxiety stem from misplaced, misdirected attention. Like Peter who began well when walking on water, we begin to sink and panic when our attention is drawn from the Lord to our immediate surroundings (Matt. 14:22-33). Jesus knows this about us, which is why He constantly called the attention of the disciples back to Himself and His attentive care when He noted their wandering gazes. In the Sermon on the Mount, Jesus directed the gaze of His listeners to the

---

5. Keller, Phillip. *A Shepherd Looks at Psalm 23*, (Grand Rapids: Zondervan, 1977), 93.

native flora by the Sea of Galilee (Matt. 6:26-31). Pointing out the delicate lilies, the birds, and the grass, Jesus reminded His listeners that the same God who delights to care for fleeting flowers cares far more attentively for His children. After bidding them use their senses and their minds to consider, He leaves no question as to the meaning of the lesson, exclaiming to them, "Fear not, little flock, for it is your Father's good pleasure to give you the kingdom!" (Luke 12:32). He bids us to notice Him as He notices us. He invites us to pay attention to the one who pays careful attention to us.

Our attentive God commands our attention (Matt. 17:5; Mark 9:7; Luke 9:35). The one whose eyes are ever upon us asks us to direct our eyes to Him (Ps. 121:1; Isa. 45:22). David exclaims, "The eyes of the LORD are toward the righteous and his ears toward their cry" (Ps. 34:15). Oh, that we would be postured toward the one so postured towards us.

## Chapter Two

# Attention Leads to Adoration

If I had a dollar for every time I have heard the phrase, "Mom, look at me!" I would be richer than Melinda Gates. Children innately make the critical connection between attention and adoration that adults tend to miss. Even as they sit in a playroom full of toys purchased for them by their hard-working parents, children hunger for the affirmation of their parents' love which is communicated through attention. This is yet another facet to the wisdom Jesus communicated to His disciples when He said, "Truly, I say to you, unless you turn and become like children, you will never enter the kingdom of heaven" (Matt. 18:3).

In the Sermon on the Mount, Jesus explicitly states the inherent connection between affection and attention. After addressing the corrosive spiritual danger of treasuring corruptible earthly goods, Jesus explains the reasoning underneath His argument: "For where your treasure is, there your heart will also be. The eye is the lamp of the body. So, if your eye is healthy, your whole body will be full of light, but if your eye is bad, your whole body will be full of darkness" (Matt. 6:21-23a).

Jesus shows the relationship between affection and attention almost as a feedback mechanism. Where our hearts have set their affection, they will set their attention. Likewise, the more we set our attention on something, the more our affections for it will increase. Put succinctly, we become what we behold, whether for ill or for good. As Scottish theologian Henry Scougal wrote to a friend new to the faith, "The worth and excellency of a soul is to be measured by the object of its love."[1] The objects of our attention shape our souls. Scougal continues saying, "Love is the greatest and most excellent thing of which we can be masters. It is folly to bestow it unworthily."[2] Well-placed attention flows from well-placed affection.

## The Shaping Power of Attention

If you had told me twenty years ago that I would become a mother who loved baseball, I would have laughed in your face. I grew up as a soccer player and was quick to shame baseball for its seeming slowness. The few times I went to MLB games, I went for the snacks and the people watching. I continued in this vein until I had a child who loved baseball. Years of sitting for what felt like years at each of his games and watching with fixed attention have slowly shaped my affection. I have become *that* baseball momma. I choose to go to practices and never want to miss a game. I even know how to properly keep score! While this is a silly example where the stakes are low, it illustrates the powerful shaping force of attention.

The objects of our attention can either ennoble us or enslave us. Love set on the one who is worthy of it and can bear the weight of its expectation lifts our souls. Love set on lesser beings sets a snare for our souls. King David, who knew a thing or two about the dangers of misplaced affection, warned God's people, "The sorrows of those who run after another god shall multiply" (Ps.16:4). Juxtaposed with this multiplied sorrow are

---

1. Henry Scougal, *The Life of God in the Soul of Man*, (Wheaton: Crossway, 2022), 71.

2. Ibid, 73.

the "fullness of joy" and "pleasures forevermore" to be found in God's presence (Ps. 16: 11).

The vital connection between attention and affection is a thread laced throughout the entirety of the Scriptures. Affection and attention misplaced on dead idols deaden the hearts of worshipers, whereas affection and attention well-placed on the living God enliven the hearts of the worshiper. The psalmist noted, "Their idols are silver and gold, the work of human hands. They have mouths but do not speak; eyes, but do not see…. Those who make them become like them; so do all who trust in them" (Ps. 115: 4-5; 8). When writing to encourage the hearts of the Corinthian believers, the apostle Paul uses the same concept of beholding and becoming, this time in the positive light: "And we all, with unveiled face, beholding the glory of the Lord, are being transformed into the same image from one degree of glory to another. For this comes from the Lord who is the Spirit" (2 Cor. 3:18).

Nearness leads to likeness. We take on the mannerisms and even the affections of those with whom we spend the bulk of our time. In the words of James K.A. Smith, "Jesus is a teacher who doesn't just form our intellect but forms our very loves."[3]

## The Beam of Our Attention

The image of attention as a powerful beam or spotlight helps us visualize something that is hard to measure, describe, or quantify. After all, there aren't tools or gadgets to help us measure the purity or power of the attention we are giving or receiving. Yet, we all know how loved we feel when someone is giving us their full and undivided attention; we also know all too well how the inverse feels. If attention communicates affection, then inattention communicates a clear lack thereof.

We live in a culture largely known for its short attention spans and its panoply of distractions. In such a culture, the

---

3. James K.A. Smith, *You are What You Love,* (Grand Rapids: Brazos Press, 2016), 2.

beam of our attention is powerful evidence of our affection. If you want to know where your affections lie, follow the beam of your attention, both physically and spiritually. Where and how do you spend your time, talents, and treasures? What do you find yourself thinking about when you have free time? Where do your daydreams run?

## The Beam of His Attention

Thankfully, the beams of attention and affection don't begin with us. We are not called to create them but rather to receive and reflect the beams of affection and attention which find their source in our Triune God. The apostle John understood that love doesn't begin with us. He reminded the early church: "In this is love, not that we have loved God but that he has loved us and sent his Son to be the propitiation for our sins" (1 John 4:10). The beam of God's affective attention is meant to move through us to others. John continues, "Beloved, if God so loved us, we also ought to love one another" (1 John 4:11).

Long before Christ became incarnate, we see the beam of God's attention upon His creation. God punctuated each day of His creative work with a delighted, "Good!", yet He reserved His sole "Very good!" for His image bearers (Gen. 1–2). After falling into sin, Adam and Eve couldn't bear the sightlines of their creator without hiding and shame, aware as they were of their sin and failure. Yet, that did not stop God from gazing at His created ones with care. Through the covenants, God promises to love and provide for a people. His *hesed*, His covenant love, focuses His attention on His people even though they are impure and undeserving of such purity of love.

The book of Deuteronomy features multiple speeches Moses prepared for the Israelites who were preparing to move into the promised land. Moses, as any good leader, felt it expedient to remind God's people who their God was and who they were in relation to Him. In one of these powerful speeches, Moses says the following:

> For you are a people holy to the LORD your God (ESV). The LORD your God has chosen you to be a people for his treasured possession, out of all the peoples who are on the face of the earth. It was not because you were more in number than any other people that the LORD set his love on you and chose you, for you were the fewest of all peoples, but it is because the LORD loves you and is keeping the oath that he swore to your fathers. (Deut. 7:6-8a)

Moses reminds the Israelites that God loves them because He chose to set His love upon them. God directs the beam of His affection to them because He chooses to do so, not because of any merit of their own. Later, the prophets seek to reclaim the attention of God's stiff-necked, idol-chasing people, begging them to return their gaze to the one who sees them (Zech. 1:3; Mal. 3:7; Hosea 11:5). As bent as God was on loving them, so bent was the gaze of God's people in turning from Him.

Yet, God set His gaze on His people in a tangible way through the incarnation of the Second Person of the Trinity. The Gospel of John so powerfully captures the reality that He who lived from eternity in the perfect gaze of the Father became man and offered the light of His gaze to us:

> The true light, which gives light to everyone, was coming into the world. He was in the world, and the world was made through him, yet the world did not know him. He came to his own, and his own people did not receive him. But to all who did receive him, who believed in his name, he gave the right to become children of God. (John 1:9-12)

When we read through the Gospels, we see Christ who consistently focused the beams of attention on whomever was set before Him. A poor widow. A wealthy, woeful centurion. A pack of crazy kids. A crowd of hungry paupers. A suspect tax collector. Christ was able to radiate such focused attention because He always lived under the beams of His heavenly Father. The beams of God's love perpetually warmed the Son.

Yet, in those painful hours on that horrible hill, the beam of the Father's favor turned away from the Son. Through the life, death, and resurrection of Christ, the beam of attention which the perfect Son deserved has been made available to all who would trust in Him. Believers are invited to live under the gaze of their good Father. Martin Luther captured the incredible shaping power of the beam of God's love, saying, "The love of God does not find, but creates, that which is pleasing to it."[4]

## The Case for Considering

Life between Christ's first coming and His second coming is, among other things, a battleground for our attention and affection. James K. A. Smith writes that "discipleship…is a way to curate your heart, to be attentive to and intentional about what you love."[5] Christian discipleship begins at the level of our attention and our affection. The Enemy of God can do nothing to snatch us from the Father's hand, but he will do everything to distract us from His gaze (John 10:28). Thus, we ought not be surprised at how many times the writers of the New Testament call us to consider and to look again at Christ and His work on the cross. The battle for our hearts often begins with our eyes.

The Greek word *katanoeo*, which is often translated "to consider," shows up fourteen times in the New Testament. Taken at face value, that may not seem like a huge deal; however, its range of meaning helps as we think about the significance of looking again at Jesus. *Katanoeo* literally means

---

4. Luther, Martin. *Heidelberg Disputation*. Thesis 28.

5. Smith, James K.A. *You are What You Love*, (Grand Rapids: Brazos Press, 2016), 2.

"to think from up to down," "to carefully consider," and to "concentrate by focusing one's attention."[6]

William Barclay writes extensively about the meaning of this word:

> Now this word does not mean simply to look at or to notice a thing. Anyone can look at a thing or notice it without in any sense really seeing it. The word means to fix the attention on something in such a way that the inner meaning of the thing, the lesson that the thing is designed to teach, may be learned... If we are ever to learn Christian truth, a lack-lustre, disinterested, detached glance is never enough; there must be a concentrated gaze in which we gird up the loins of the mind in a determined effort to see its meaning for us.[7]

Jesus used this word in His well-known call to "Consider the ravens" and "Consider the lilies" (Luke 12:24; 27). Just as He invited us to look carefully and attentively with our physical eyes that we might learn an important spiritual lesson, other writers of the New Testament invite us to look at and consider Jesus carefully. The writer of Hebrews tells the Jewish Christians, "Therefore, holy brothers, you who share in a heavenly calling, consider Jesus, the apostle and high priest of our confession" (Heb. 3:1).

While we might expect the New Testament writers to bid us consider Christ, they also invite us to consider our own weakness and inability. When the apostle Paul wrote about the faith of Abraham, he used this word multiple times. Abraham *considered* both "his own body, which was as good as dead" and "the barrenness of Sarah's womb" (Rom. 4:19). Thankfully, he did not stop there. He moved his gaze from the grim realities of their situation and circumstances to set his hope and gaze

---

6. https://biblehub.com/greek/2657.htm

7. Barclay, William. *The Letter to the Hebrews*. (Philadelphia: Westminster Press, 1955), 23.

on the character of God. Paul continues, writing that Abraham "grew strong in faith as he gave glory to God, fully convinced that God was able to do what he had promised" (Rom. 4:20-21).

When we look carefully at our own selves and circumstances, we are often compelled to look at Christ. As C.H. Spurgeon understands, "Your extremity is God's opportunity."[8] When considering ourselves or our circumstances, we would do well to take the advice of another Scottish pastor. Robert Murray McCheyne wisely wrote, "For every look at yourself, take ten looks at Christ."[9]

Careful consideration plays a crucial role in the life of faith. J.I. Packer once noted that a complex subject requires a complex knowing. He writes, "Knowledge of something abstract, like a language, is acquired by learning…But when one gets to living things, knowing them becomes a good deal more complicated."[10] Knowledge of the living God requires the complex understanding that comes from wholehearted attention and careful considering (and re-considering).

## Cultivating Attention

Hopefully, your heart is stirred by the living and active Word of God to consider Christ. However, if you are anything like me, you may begin to wonder how one goes about practically considering Christ. It should go without saying that we cannot love a God we don't know. Thankfully, our God wants to be known and reveals Himself to us.

God reveals Himself to us through His Word and by His Spirit; thus, we have the full counsel of the Scriptures to help us focus our attention upon Christ. An obvious place to start concentrating our coupled attention and affection on Christ is

---

8. Spurgeon, C.H. "Man's Extremity, God's Opportunity" https://www.spurgeon.org/resource-library/sermons/mans-extremity-gods-opportunity/#flipbook/

9. Bonar, Andrew. *Memoir & Remains of Robert Murray M'Cheyne*, (Edinburgh: Banner of Truth, 1966), 293.

10. Packer, J.I. *Knowing God*, (Downers Grove: IVP, 1973), 30.

by reading and meditating upon the gospel accounts which tell of His life on earth as the incarnate one. While the Gospels are a great starting point, they are far from the only place to consider Christ. Jesus stunned two discouraged disciples one day as they were walking home from Jerusalem on the days following His death. "Beginning with Moses and all the Prophets, he interpreted to them in all the Scriptures the things concerning himself" (Luke 24:27). When we realize what Jesus is saying, our hearts ought to burn with the disciples on the road to Emmaus (Luke 24:32). The entirety of Scripture points us to Christ. Thus, when we study the Law or the Prophets or the wisdom books or the Psalms, we can practice considering Christ.

Reading the Scriptures is not like reading another book. Since the Scriptures are living and active God-breathed words, the Scriptures read us while we read them (Heb. 4:12-13; 2 Tim. 3:16). The Holy Spirit illuminates to us the realities that God wants to show us while also illuminating our own hearts (1 Thess. 1:5; 1 Cor. 2:10-12). Theologians speak of the Holy Spirit as dwelling in double-depth: He is both deep within God and deep within the children of God.[11] As such, the Spirit facilitates and focuses our faith as we seek to know Christ through the Word. We need God to see God, and the Third Person of the Trinity focuses the beam of our attention on the person of Christ.

Our intake of the Word, through reading, studying, and meditation, rightly stirs our hearts to want to pray—which is a second significant way to learn to consider Christ with our full attention. Whereas Israel trekked to the Temple to pray on a regular basis, believers in Christ always have unparalleled access to God (Ps. 122:1; 1 Kings 8:21-29). Whereas Israel could only approach God through the continual offering of the blood of animal sacrifices, we approach Christ confidently

---

11. Sanders, Fred. *The Holy Spirit: An Introduction*, (Wheaton: Crossway, 2023), 12-13.

through His better blood, shed once for all (Heb. 4:16; 10:4,12). The writer of Hebrews reminded the Jewish believers of the wonder of their full access to God through Christ and bid them use it!

Here again, we are indebted to the help of the Holy Spirit. The Spirit helps us in our weakness, for we often don't know what to pray (Rom. 8:26). Dwelling at double-depth, as we learned, the Spirit knows both the parts of our hearts we don't even know and the will of God (Rom. 8:27). He does the wonderful work of interceding for us and through us so that we might be conformed to the likeness of the Son (Rom 8:29). In his letter to the Ephesians, the apostle Paul makes another critical connection between our prayers and the Spirit of God. He reminds them to keep "praying at all times in the Spirit, with all prayer and supplication" and bids them to "keep alert with all perseverance, making supplication for all the saints" (Eph. 6:18).

We do not have time to fully unpack the rich realities of prayer in the life of a believer. Yet, I would be remiss if I didn't highlight prayer as a wonderfully broad window through which we are invited to train our attention towards Christ. Simone Weil uses the language of attention to describe prayer when she writes the following: "Prayer consists of attention…It is the orientation of all the attention of which the soul is capable toward God. The quality of the attention counts for much in the quality of prayer."[12]

The heart of prayer is turning the beam of our attention towards the one who rightly deserves it. Prayer also affords us the opportunity to enjoy and be transformed by the loving gaze of the Father. Such a focusing of our attention requires both natural power and supernatural help. We are called to do our part in setting ruts of righteousness through the habits of holiness and the disciplines of grace even as our Triune God helps us. The Spirit indwelling aids our prayers as the Son

---

12. Weil, Simone. *Waiting for God,* (New York: Harper & Row, 1951), 105.

intercedes for us Himself that the Father might grant us all we need to turn our gaze towards our Triune God (Heb. 7:25; Eph. 2:14-19).

## Looking At Versus Looking Through

When I first heard about Carthusian monks, I found myself intrigued (perhaps because I am an introvert living in an extroverted calling). As I investigated this order of Catholic monks and nuns founded in the mountains of France over a thousand years ago, my shock transmuted into stunned awe. The life of an ordinary monk strikes us as strange, but the life of Carthusian monks seems other-worldly. Carthusian monks spend most of their day as literal hermits in their individual cells, only leaving their modest rooms for three short masses a day and for a walk once a week. My first thought after my brief exploration of this order was that maybe I was not as introverted as I previously thought! My second, more serious, query was, "Is this the only path to seriously consider Christ?"

The Scriptures do, indeed, call us to "pray without ceasing" and "take captive every thought to the obedience of Christ" (1 Thess. 5:17; 2 Cor. 10:5); however, the varied life of the early church clearly shows that there is a way to obey these commands without living in a hermitage. The Carthusians would agree. They exist so that, always, somewhere in this world, someone is interceding for our world and meditating upon Christ. While I appreciate their unique service, I hunger for practical ways to consider Christ as I drive carpools, counsel women, and walk my dogs.

As much as I might daydream about a day alone in a quiet cell, the Lord has not called me to a quiet hermitage. He has given me a husband to love, serve, and follow. Together, we have three anything-but-quiet boys and seek to serve the local church. Learning to look through the people around me back to God helps me to consider Christ in the throes of this glorious (and often chaotic) calling.

As we have seen, soul and sight are inextricably tied together. We are supposed to look *through* the experiences of our everyday lives back to the God who called us to them. Our physical realities and our present company are meant to be windows through which we can better understand, experience, and worship the God who stands behind and before all of creation. The smile of an infant, the breath-stopping beauty of the Grand Canyon, the laughter shared over a family meal: these are intended to stir our hearts to consider again our creator. Even the circumstances which cause us to sigh and to cry can be windows back to the heart of God. Discomfort and disease remind us that we are exiles who aren't home yet and press us into the God of all comforts and the Father of mercies (2 Cor. 1:3).

These words may sound simple and stirring, but the actual practice of looking through created things back to the creator can be quite difficult. C.S. Lewis offers a helpful image that captures the work involved in considering Christ amid the circumstances of our daily lives. In the book *Letters to Malcolm: Chiefly on Prayer*, he describes his attempt "to make every pleasure into a channel of adoration"[13] and likens this personal practice to climbing up the sunbeams towards the sun: "Gratitude exclaims . . . 'How good of God to give me this.' Adoration says, 'What must be the quality of that Being whose far-off and momentary coruscations are like this!' One's mind runs back up the sunbeam to the sun."[14]

To Lewis' helpful image of climbing up the sunbeam I would add a counterpart for sorrows: slide down your sorrows into the arms of your Savior. Sorrows don't feel like sunbeams which require ascent to find God, they often feel like scary slides of descent. Yet, at the base of every sorrow, we will find a suffering Savior, "a man of sorrows" who was well-acquainted

---

13. Lewis, C.S. *Letters to Malcolm: Chiefly on Prayer*. (London: William Collins, 1964), 120.

14. Ibid, 121.

with grief (Isa. 53:3). When sorrows seem to have us sliding in descent, we can remember the words of Corrie ten Boom who lived through the Holocaust to say with confidence, "There is no pit so deep that God's love is not deeper still."[15] We look through both our joys and our sorrow to see our Savior with scarred hands working all things together for our good (Rom. 8:28).

On my best days, my eyes join my soul in looking for life from the life-giver who stands behind and underneath the realities of my life. Interruptions to my plans for the day can be seen as course corrections from a well-intended heavenly Father. My children's meltdowns can be seen as windows into their needs rather than weights to slow me down. Unfortunately, the inverse is also true. When my soul grows weary, my eyes tend to follow suit. My eyes and soul, that tired pair, quickly lose their farther, deeper focus. Then, I begin to look *at* rather than *through*.

When our eyes begin to look *at* rather than seeing *through*, our souls need a fresh check-in with the gentle physician. When our focus becomes shortened, we need help lifting our gazes again to the Lord (Ps. 121:1). One day we will see Him constantly and clearly, but until then, one practical way to practice considering Christ is to learn to look *through* rather than *at* our present company and circumstances (1 John 3:2 and 1 Cor.13:12).

## Attention Leads to Obedience

We have spent the greater portion of this chapter looking at the God-intended connection between attention and affection. We have explored some of the commands to carefully consider Christ and explored prayer and the Word of God, both aided by the indwelling Spirit of God, as two significant pathways towards doing so. I want to land our chapter by exploring

---

15. Ten Boom, Corrie. *The Hiding Place*. (Grand Rapids: Chosen Books, 1971), 197.

obedience as the appropriate end to which attention and affection run.

Obedience has run upon hard times in our postmodern culture. Somehow, the world, the flesh, and the devil have twisted and contorted obedience, a glorious end, into a bad word; however, biblically speaking, obedience is our right response to attention fixed on Christ and affections warmed by Christ. God never intended us to simply stare and be stirred; He means that we would follow Him. Here we find another feedback loop: focused attention and affection lead to obedience which leads to greater attention and focus.

When writing to the early church in Jerusalem, James pointed out how unnatural it was to look at and listen to God without moving toward obedience. As you read the following verses, listen for language of attention and obedience:

> But be doers of the word, and not hearers only, deceiving yourselves. For if anyone is a hearer of the word and not a doer, he is like a man who looks intently at his natural face in a mirror. For he looks at himself and goes away and at once forgets what he was like. But the one who looks into the perfect law, the law of liberty, and perseveres, being no hearer who forgets but a doer who acts, he will be blessed in his doing. (James 1:22-25)

Our attention (our listening and looking, as mentioned by James) ought to lead to blessed obedience. If it doesn't, perhaps we are not truly paying attention or seeing rightly. Did you hear the affection James assumed we should have for the law? James called God's commands, "the perfect law, the law of liberty," which is a far cry from the postmodern idea of law. We wrongly assume that law enslaves, but it frees us to live at liberty.

The apostle John sings from the same songbook regarding affection, attention, and obedience. He writes, "By this we know that we love the children of God, when we love God and obey his commandments. For this is the love of God, that we keep his commandants. And his commandments are not burdensome" (1 John 5:2-3).

Soren Kierkegaard draws a helpful distinction between admirers and followers of Christ, one that means even more in a culture where we use the word "follower" ubiquitously and lightly. According to Kierkegaard, "An admirer…keeps himself personally detached. He fails to see that what is admired involves a claim upon him."[16] He goes on to say the following convicting words about admirers of Christ:

> The admirer never makes any true sacrifices. He always plays it safe. Though in word he is inexhaustible about how highly he prizes Christ, he renounces nothing, will not reconstruct his life, and will not let his life express what it is he supposedly admires. Not so the follower. No, No. The follower aspires with all his strength to be what he admires.[17]

God wants followers who obey Him, not merely admirers who appreciate Him. When God has our attention, He grows our affection. Growing affection for God evidences itself through increasing glad obedience to God. All throughout this cycle, God receives glory as we receive joy.

---

16. Kierkegaard, Soren. *Bread & Wine: Readings for Lent and Easter*, (Maryknoll: Orbis Books, 2003), 56.

17. Ibid, 60.

# Chapter Three

# Inattention and Alloyed Attention

## Divided Attention

I thought I was adept at multitasking in college. My friends and I would drag blankets out to the grassy quad in the middle of campus toting books and assignments in one hand and frisbees and radios in the other (yes, I went to college with the dinosaurs and before cell phones). I'd sit with an English novel the size of a cinder block on my lap, reading the same sentence twenty times as frisbees whirred past my head and friends chatted all around me. You can imagine how much work we accomplished on those picnic blankets. You can't blame us for trying. We didn't have access to the neurological discoveries that have busted the myth of multitasking.

As much as we would like to pat ourselves on the back for multitasking skills, our brains tell a very different story. When we think we are managing multiple tasks at once, we are rapidly switching between two different neural networks operating mostly in the subconscious regions of our brain.[1]

---

1. In his book *The Organized Mind: Thinking Straight in the Age of Information Overload*, Daniel Levitin devotes multiple chapters to explaining the various attention systems in the human brain. While Levitin is not

Much of our mental exhaustion and decision-making fatigue results from our brain cells being tired from overly operating the switch between the two systems. Our brains are not wired for doing two things at once. We were created for focused attention: one task—or one person—at a time.

There are now entire books dedicated to fighting inattention and distraction from a purely neurobiological approach.

While these books might help us to better use our brains to cultivate optimal attention and focus, they fail to understand that our problem goes far deeper than divided attention and splintered focus. Our divided attention stems from our divided hearts.

## Divided Hearts

As we covered in our last chapter, Jesus understood the connection between our physical eyes and the eyes of our hearts. If the eye is the lamp of the body, then distracted eyes darting here and there reveal distracted hearts. Computers with twenty tabs reveal minds with twenty more. Gathering glances at the phone to count "likes" stem from soul glances away from God.

Our distraction problems didn't begin in an Apple Store, they originated in a garden. The God who created us for Himself and created a world for us wired us for attention. He intended that we would use both the intricate bodies He designed and the souls He created in His image for His glory and our good (Gen. 1:26-27). Adam and Eve were created for God and given a garden to cultivate and keep. They had the privilege of connection to their creator, who, it seems, was in the habit of walking in the garden with them (Gen. 3:8). They had animals to name and lands to tame (Gen. 2:19-20).

---

coming from the perspective of Christian faith, his explanations of recent neurobiological discoveries are helpful. As those who know that we have been intimately and intricately wired by our creator, such complex systems which puzzle evolutionary biologists, only affirm what we already know!

All the language loaded into the beginning of the book of beginnings screams of a God who intended us to employ all our senses in worship and service to Him. Before the fall, worship wasn't divided. Adam and Eve worshiped and enjoyed God as they did whatever was set before them with their whole hearts. The eyes of their hearts were upon God even when their physical eyes were busy with other tasks. Shalom was their setting, until everything was shattered by sin.

When the seat of our souls shifted from God to self, Adam and Eve saw things differently. "Then the eyes of both were opened, and they knew that they were naked" is the first sentence to follow the fall (Gen. 3:7). Sin makes us see the world differently. Distortion, distraction, and division shattered the shalom.

It is sin's nature to divide and separate. Sin separates us from our God (Isa. 59:2). Sin separates us from each other (Gen. 3:12-13). Sin separates us from ourselves through shame (Gen. 3:8). Sin separates our focus and scatters our thoughts. Sin scatters, shatters, and divides that which was meant to be whole. It did so with devastating effects in the garden, and it still wreaks such havoc in our hearts today.

## David, the King of Distraction

King David has the great distinction of being known as a man after God's own heart (1 Sam.13:14). And such he was! When the bravest warriors Israel could muster were cowering in fear of Goliath, a young David showed great ferocity and faith. He didn't borrow Saul's ill-fitting armor, because his heart was armed with the reality of God's promises and provision. As a young shepherd, David spent many nights and long days paying attention to the sheep entrusted to him by his father Jesse. David's daring faith evidences his awareness that God paid attention to him and shepherded him. Fresh from the fields of his shepherding days, David showed a heart full of faith focused on God before taking down Goliath. He told the fear-shaking Saul, "The LORD who delivered me from the paw of the lion and the paw of the bear will deliver me from the hand of this Philistine" (1 Sam. 17:37).

David proved to be not only an incredible king but also an incredibly complex and honest king. Through the scores of psalms he penned, we have the privilege of peering into his soul. Even a cursory reading of his psalms and the stories recorded about his life in the Scriptures reveal the complexity of David's inner man. He was more honest with God than many of us dare to be. David knew a thing or twenty about the situations and sins that divide and distract the human heart. By God's grace, he also knew the God who continually created in him a pure, whole heart (Ps. 51:10).

The range of emotions conveyed in the psalms he crafted reveals a man who knew the human condition well. David's songs pulse with despair, grief, retribution, joy, and relief. David admits the depths of his sin and the heights of the love of God. In this chapter, we will peer together at a few psalms of David as portholes into his heart. We will begin with Psalm 86 which will serve as a springboard into two others. In all three, I believe God will have much to show us about our own divided hearts.

## Prayers for a United Heart

The concept of attention sets the backdrop for Psalm 86. David pleads for the attention of his God at the beginning, in the middle, and at the end of the song. His pleas for God's attention flow from what David knows about God's character: "For you, O Lord, are good and forgiving, abounding in steadfast love to all who call upon you" and "There is none like you among the gods, O Lord, nor are there any works like yours" (Ps. 86:5; 8). Reasoning out from God's revealed nature, David humbly asks for His attention: "Incline your ear, O LORD, and answer me, for I am poor and needy" (Ps. 86:1); "Give ear, O

Lord, to my prayer; listen to my plea for grace" (Ps. 86:6); and "Turn to me and be gracious to me (Ps. 86:16).

Scattered throughout the song, we hear snippets of the circumstances compelling David's prayers and pleas. He feels "poor and needy" (Ps. 86:1). He is crying out for God "all the day" (Ps. 86:3). "Insolent men" and "a band of ruthless men" are apparently after him (Ps. 86:14). There is much to steal his attention, yet David continually postures himself towards the presence of God. At the heart of the psalm, we see David's heart most clearly:

> Teach me your way, O Lord, that I may walk in your truth; unite my heart to fear your name. I give thanks to you, O Lord my God, with my whole heart, and I will glorify your name forever. For great is your steadfast love toward me; you have delivered my soul from the depths of Sheol (Ps. 86:11-13).

David knew from searing personal experience that distraction and divided hearts are related. Thus, he asks the Lord for a heart that is united in fear of His name (Ps. 86:11). He even anticipates God helping him offer such full-hearted devotion (Ps. 86:12). But did you catch the motivation underneath those prayers for a united, whole heart? David longs for focused concentration that stems from committed devotion to the Lord because he recognizes the greatness of God's steadfast love toward him (Ps. 86:13). When we take time to meditate upon the fact that the God of the universe directs His love and attention toward us, we long to return the favor. Love begets love. Focused attention feeds focused attention.

But the reciprocal is also true. Distracted hearts lead to distance. I cannot help but wonder if David's deep and desperate prayers for a united heart stem from his own painful experiences of a divided, distracted heart. David, of all people, knew his tendency to distraction. After all, distraction was one of the fatal steps in his rapid decline into a sin cycle that ended in adultery and murder. After the first temptation to stay home when everyone else went to war, David found himself with quite a bit of free time, as "Joab and his servants with him, and all Israel" were sent out in the "spring of the year" to advance Israel's borders (2 Sam. 11:1). One verse later, we read, "It happened, late one afternoon, when David arose from his couch and was walking on the roof of the king's house, that he saw from the roof a woman bathing: and the woman was very beautiful" (2 Sam. 11:2). You likely know David's dismal story that begins with distraction and ends with devastation.

## Divided by Sin

As we said earlier, God created us for wholeness and wholehearted devotion. After all, we were created out of the fullness of the Trinity: God the Father loving God the Son through God the Holy Spirit. We were made from His wholeness for wholeness. We were knit together body, mind, and soul. Sin bifurcates and pulls apart what God intended to be sewn seamlessly together. The world and the flesh further cut us into parts and pieces where God intended an integrated and whole soul.

The sexual revolution sold the lie that what we do with the body stays there. Promising to free people from the constraints of covenanted, committed love, it seared souls and marred minds. Pornography does the same: it sells the sinister lie that what eyes see on a screen stays two-dimensional when, in fact, it wreaks havoc in real life. While the separation of body, mind, and soul are obvious when it comes to sexual sin, the same concept applies to distraction in its more benign forms. We think that mindlessly scrolling on social media is a neutral act when, in fact, it stirs up comparison and discontentment at the soul level. On a physical level, constant scrolling on screens rewires neural pathways in the same way that addiction to substances hijack our dopamine systems. We are knit together, for better or for worse. Just as God established the physical world with laws that regulate it for our flourishing (i.e. gravity, the laws of motion, and the laws of thermodynamics), He established spiritual laws that regulate our souls. When we turn away from God and look to lesser things as a source of life, the consequences affect the whole of our lives. As goes the body, so goes the soul.

Thus, when David lost track of God's good purposes for him and lowered his eyes from gazing at God by looking lustfully upon Bathsheba, his body and soul were lowered as well. Sin led to sin. Physical distraction led to spiritual desolation. As the sin snowball grew, David's heart hardened, and his circumstances became increasingly complicated by sin.

What we learn narratively from the historic account, we hear poetically from David in Psalm 32. Samuel gives us the facts of David's fall, while David himself fills in the feelings as he remembers his descent into sin: "For when I kept silent, my bones wasted away through my groaning all day long. For day and night your hand was heavy upon me; my strength was dried up as by the heat of summer" (Ps. 32:3-4).

David's distraction led to the disintegration of his body and distance from God. If you are like me, your first response to David's massive mistakes is to put them in a category more egregious than your own (in a sort of "the bigger they are, the harder they fall" fallacy). However, what we see happening in David's life gives us insight into what happens in the microcosms of our own lives. Sin always separates. Distraction always divides. Hearts and souls follow eyes and bodies. These are spiritual laws that don't disappear simply because we don't want them to be true. We would all admit it is the height of pride for someone to declare, "Gravity doesn't apply to me;" however, when we refuse to believe we reap what we sow, we are essentially saying likewise.

Thankfully, David had a faithful friend in Nathan who loved him enough to wound him (Prov. 27:6; 2 Sam. 12:1-15). David composed this song to remember the relief of full repentance, as seen from its initial verses: "Blessed is the one whose transgression is forgiven, whose sin is covered. Blessed is the man against whom the LORD counts no iniquity and in whose spirit there is no deceit" (Ps. 32:1-2).

David offers wholehearted praise as he remembers the freedom and fullness that stemmed from admitting his divided heart. In returning to God, he was re-membered (put back together). His connection with God, with others, and within himself which his sin severed, was united through his repentance. David's remembrance of repentance in Psalm 51 provides us with a third porthole through which we may peer into his heart.

## Prayers for a Pure Heart

Whereas our previous psalm offered a generic remembrance of repentance, our present psalm was written, "When Nathan the prophet went to him, after he had gone into Bathsheba." David's first plea after he has been convicted of his heinous sin is to throw himself upon the mercy of God based on the character of God (Ps. 51:1). Seeing the filth of his sin, he cries out, "Wash me thoroughly of my iniquity, and cleanse me from my sin" (Ps. 51: 2). As the psalm continues, David's awareness of his sin seems to deepen. By the middle of the psalm, David begs God, "Create in me a clean heart, O God, and renew a right spirit within me" (Ps. 51:10). The Hebrew word *taher*, translated here as "clean," literally means "pure," whether ceremonially, physically, chemically, or morally.

I highlight the Hebrew only because Soren Kierkegaard's definition of purity of heart sheds light on the paired ideas of distraction and attention. Before reading Kierkegaard, I tended to associate purity of heart with moral purity and holiness, which is certainly an appropriate and obvious meaning. Kierkegaard's statement that "purity of heart is to will one thing"[2] helped to broaden and deepen the concept for me. Purity of heart implies single-minded devotion to the high and holy God.

Willing one thing above all else is not new to Kierkegaard; rather, this concept is laced throughout the Bible. The Lord created us to long for Him as the unifying and organizing center of our lives. In the first two commandments given through Moses to Israel, God explicitly states that He is the only rightful center (Exod. 20:1-6). David himself explores this theme in another psalm when he declares, "One thing I have asked of the LORD, that I will seek after: that I may dwell in the house of the LORD all the days of my life, to gaze upon the beauty of the LORD and to inquire in his temple" (Ps. 27:4). When He walked upon the earth, Jesus both modeled and commanded a similar singularity of desire and focus on God. He did not shy away from telling Mary that focusing on Him was "the one thing needful," the greatest necessity of her life (Luke 10:42). Similarly, in the beatitudes, Jesus declares, "Blessed are the pure in heart, for they shall see God" (Matt. 5:8). Jesus' statement stands in perfect alignment with God's promise through the prophet Jeremiah: "Then you will call upon me and come and pray to me, and I will hear you. You will seek me and find me, when you seek me with all your heart" (Jer. 29:12-13).

Taken together, the whole counsel of Scripture invites us to seek God wholeheartedly. David's plea for a pure heart is a cry for a unified and unifying focus on God. Distraction and idolatry shattered both his life and his focus; repentance and worship were the paths back to wholeness. King David's own psalms (Pss. 86, 32, and 51) helped us address distraction, but now we must explore two other enemies of a unified heart: our alloyed and intermittent attention.

---

2. Kierkegaard, Soren. *Purity of Heart is to Will One Thing*, (Radford: A & D Publishing, 2008), Introduction.

## Alloyed Attention

The sin of inattention to our Triune God can wear a few different sets of clothes: it can look like the obvious distraction and inattention we have seen in the life of David, but it can also look like alloyed or intermittent attention. Even if we don't think much about alloys (an alloy is a mixture of two metals), we are likely still prone to alloyed attention (the diluting of our attention to God by mixing it with inattention or wrong motives for attention).

If David taught us about distraction, ancient Israel teaches us about alloyed attention. While they had moments of outright distraction and disobedience like their worshiping of the golden calf, the ancient Israelites also lived in long stretches of alloyed attention and half-hearted obedience. Israel felt a sense of security in their rote obedience and half-hearted attention; thus, God sent the prophets to expose their mediocrity and call them back to adoring attention to Him. Speaking through the prophet Isaiah, God lamented, saying, "This people draw near with their mouth and honor me with their lips, while their hearts are far from me" (Isa. 29:13). God expressed a similar sentiment through the prophet Ezekiel, "And they come to you as people come, …and they hear what you say but they will not do it" (Ezek. 33:31). In these and many other instances addressed through the prophets, God's people are not blatantly disobedient. They are showing up, going through the motions, practicing a half-hearted rote obedience; however, their attention is hollow rather than hallowed. Through the prophets' words, we learn that God doesn't want alloyed attention, but wholehearted worship.

In the last book of the Bible, we hear a similar cry for hearty attention. God, speaking through the exiled apostle John, writes to the Church in Ephesus, "But I have this against you, that you have abandoned the love you had at first" (Rev. 2:4). In the preceding verse, God noted the patient endurance of the saints at Ephesus, so we know that they were not walking in distraction or disobedience; yet God wants more than mere obedience (Rev. 2:3). Here we see that God wants wholehearted obedience compelled by love, affection, and wonder. He won't merely have our bodies or our minds, He would have all of us. As Jesus clearly stated when asked about the greatest commandment, "You shall love the Lord your God with all your heart and with all your soul and with all your mind" (Matt. 22:37).

Using Kierkegaard's definition of purity of heart, alloyed attention is wanting Christ among many other things. Full attention on Christ seeks Christ alone, while alloyed attention seeks Christ plus various sundry things. Idolatry is looking for life apart from Christ, but it also looking for life in Christ in addition to other things. Christ plus marriage, Christ plus a new house, Christ plus successful ministry, or any other Christ plus formula is evidence of alloyed attention towards God.

## Intermittent Attention

The problem of intermittent attention is a close cousin of alloyed attention. With intermittent attention, we begin with wholehearted attention but are soon buffeted by distraction or fear. We start with eyes fixed on the author and perfecter of our faith until the beam of our gaze is broken by glances all around us. The life of the apostle Peter provides us with honest examples of the dangers of intermittent attention. Ever the impetuous one, Peter lived with his whole heart, for good or ill. While other disciples were slower to decide, Peter literally jumped headlong into situations and circumstances with Jesus.

Directly after Jesus commanded the attention of the crowds by feeding them miraculously from five loaves and two fish, we find Peter in his own battle with attention and inattention (Matt. 14). Jesus, having sent the disciples on in the boat ahead of Him, walked towards his boat-bound disciples on the water. Upon seeing Him, Peter said, "Lord, if it is you, command me to come to you on the water," to which Jesus replied, "Come"

(Matt. 14:28-29). All went well at first. Peter began with his attention fixed on Jesus (Matt. 14:29). However, Matthew notes, "But when he saw the wind, he was afraid, and beginning to sink he cried out, "Lord, save me" (Matt. 14:30). While this passage is primarily about doubt versus faith, attention plays a crucial role in the ensuing battle.

We don't have actual experiences of water-walking like Peter, but we can understand his battle. When our eyes are fixed on Jesus, our faith is focused on its proper object. We often begin well, venturing out upon our own proverbial waters, staring at our Savior. Like Peter, we start to waver when we glance at our circumstances or navel-gaze at ourselves. Intermittent attention affects our ability to walk in full and free obedience to Jesus.

Perhaps we sense God inviting us to start a small business, initiate toward a nonbelieving friend, or give generously to a missionary couple. We respond in faith, confident that God will give us what we need to honor Him in our decided actions. All goes swimmingly until we turn our attention to the competition, the raised eyebrows, or the stacking bills. Suddenly, we are not so sure anymore. What began as a beam of focused attention has become scattershot by fear, lies, and doubts. Our physical sight begins to lead our spiritual sight away from God and His promises.

Jesus comes at the same reality from the positive angle in the Sermon on the Mount. I find it interesting how much sensory language Jesus employs in this extended time of teaching about life in the kingdom of God. The repetition of the phrases, "You have heard it said…But I say to you" invokes a deeper listening in his audience (Matt. 5:21-22, 27-28, 31-32, 33-34, 38-30, 43-44). Jesus' example of salt and light begs his hearers to experience with their whole beings the deep realities Jesus unpacks. Jesus' use of the imperatives, "Look at the birds of the air" and "Consider the lilies of the field" calls His people to a physical sight that is to inform their spiritual sight of Him (Matt. 6:26-34). The same senses that can pull our attention away from God can help us strengthen our attention towards Him.

The one who created our senses and wired us for embodied experience expects us to use those senses to strengthen our faith. The enemy seeks to hijack those self-same senses to destabilize and distract our faith, just as he did at the dawn of creation.

## The Whole Christ

As Paul describes succinctly in the first chapter of Romans, idolatry is lowering both our gaze and worship from creator to created things (Rom. 1:18-25). Martin Luther captured this concept through a Latin phrase and its accompanying visual picture: sin makes us *incurvatus in se* (curved in ourselves). Our hearts, our gazes, and our affections are warped by sin, and the gospel is the only way for them to be straightened. In our sin, we do not see our God, ourselves, or our world as we ought. Through the gospel, our spiritual sight is restored. As the apostle Paul powerfully writes, "For God, who said, 'Let light shine out of darkness,' has shone in our hearts to give the light of the knowledge of the glory of God in the face of Jesus Christ" (2 Cor. 4:6).

The incarnate Christ, the Second Person of the Trinity, never succumbed to idolatry. He only had eyes for the Father; His gaze was fixed on Him. The busyness and chaos of our broken world might have had Jesus' glance, but they never grabbed His gaze. To borrow another Reformation phrase, Christ lived *coram deo* (before the face, under the gaze of God). In the words of R.C. Sproul, "To live *coram Deo* is to live one's entire life in the presence of God, under the authority of God, to the glory of God."[3] In word and deed, Christ consistently lived the whole life that God intended for us. As the second and better Adam, He did what the first Adam and every subsequent human failed

---

3. Sproul, R.C. "What does Coram Deo Mean?" (https://www.ligonier.org/learn/articles/what-does-coram-deo-mean).

to do (Rom. 5:12-21). Whereas Adam and Eve averted the gaze of their soul to lesser, created things, Christ lifted His eyes ever to the Father. Whereas Adam and Eve became distracted and divided by sin, Christ remained wholehearted.

Yet, as Christ took upon Himself the punishment for our sin, the Father turned His face away from the Son. His body was shattered and the loving gaze of the Father over Him was scattered. He chose this end that we might know the gaze of the Father and learn to love Him rightly. I love Jesus' words to Mary after she found Him risen from the dead, "Do not cling to me, for I have not ascended to the Father, but go to my brothers and say to them, 'I am ascending to my Father and your Father, to my God and your God" (John 20:17). Did you catch those last two descriptors of God ("My Father and your Father" and "My God and your God?")? Jesus died that we might join Him in the *coram deo* life. When He ascended to the Father, He sent the Third Person of the Trinity, the Holy Spirit, to ignite the church (quite literally, if you read Acts 2) and indwell His people.

## The Indwelling Spirit

Christ's life, death, resurrection, and ascension to the Father saved us from the power and penalty of sin; however, we are not yet removed from the presence of sin. Though we know how the battle will end, the flesh and the Spirit continue to battle in the hearts of believers (Gal. 5:16-26). We grow in Christ the same way we came to Christ initially: through repentance and faith. Our initial repentance (in which the Spirit is always prior) marks our justification, but our ongoing repentance and returning to Christ enables our sanctification (in which the Spirit is also always prior). As Martin Luther wrote in the first of his Ninety-Five Theses which propelled the Protestant Reformation, "When our Lord and Master Jesus Christ said, 'Repent,' he willed the entire life of believers to be one of repentance."[4]

Nearly as often as we breath, we need to repent and return to the Lord. Our spiritual and physical eyes lose their focus. Our hearts become splintered and scattered. Even when we genuinely desire that purity of heart which is to will one thing, we find an unseen war waging within us (Rom. 7:21-24). Thankfully, we are not alone in this battle for our attention and our affection. The indwelling Third Person of the Trinity loves to convict us and return our gaze to our God upon whom it rightfully belongs (John 16:8-11).

The Holy Spirit loves to lead us out of ourselves and focus our attention on Christ. Puritan Thomas Goodwin writes the following about the Holy Spirit: "He is that Person that leadeth us out of ourselves unto the grace of God the Father, and the peace and satisfaction made by Jesus Christ."[5]

In Chapter One, we spent time fixing our attention on our attentive God. We explored the myriad ways God sees, hears, and knows His people as the transcendent yet immanent God of the universe. In Chapter Two, we investigated the connection between attention and affection and remembered how we must consider (and keep considering) Christ. In this chapter, we did the uncomfortable, but important work of addressing our inattention, alloyed, and intermittent attention. Hopefully, we saw not only our sin, but also our Savior more clearly. In the next chapter, we will explore the elements of living a life of focused faith.

---

4. https://www.luther.de/en/95thesen.html

5. Goodwin, Thomas. *An Exposition of the Epistle to the Ephesians, vol. 1, Works of Thomas Goodwin* (Edinburgh: James Nichol, 1861), 21.

# Chapter Four

# Faith and Focus

As a biology major, I spent far too much time sitting in formaldehyde-smelling labs looking through microscopes. I think my neck still bears the scars of sitting scrunched up straining to see diatoms and cross-sections of cells. I am embarrassed to admit that it took an entire semester of Microbiology for me to confess to my professor that I did not know how to properly bring the slides into focus. Thankfully, my professor met my clumsy confession with grace and practical aid. At first, it took great effort and concentration to achieve the necessary balance between the gross and fine adjustment knobs. Eventually, when I got the hang of it, a whole new world opened to me. While I ended up leaving behind labs and microscopes, I am indebted to the lesson of learning how to bring things into focus.

When it comes to learning how to spiritually focus, I wish it were as simple as learning to master two knobs. But, as we said before, the more complex the subject matter, the more complex the knowing. In this chapter, we will spend time exploring the art of focusing our spiritual sight through faith. The writer of Hebrews understood the central significance of faith to the Christian life. Faith is the currency of the kingdom; without faith, it is impossible to please God (Heb. 11:6). Faith requires the focus of our spiritual sight on the Triune God, and such focus and concentration are strengthened through the practice of holy habits enabled by the help of our God.

## The Art of Paying Attention

From time to time, I substitute teach for the small Christian school my children attended in their early years. This act, while putting a little money in my pocket, reminds me regularly that teachers are incredible, essential, and courageous (and that I did not, in fact, miss my calling). While teachers' classrooms and routines are as diverse as they are, there is one thing I have learned to expect: each teacher has a clear and high standard of what concentration looks like. In one classroom, the mere mention of the word "SLANT" changed everything. In a moment, the children would respond in unison, "Sit up; Lean forward; Ask and answer questions; Nod your head and Track the speaker." They simultaneously straightened their posture, silenced their chattering, and set their eyes on me.

I tried it at home but was not met with the same response, which only reiterated my belief that teachers are incredible. They take a classroom chock full of children whose brains are still developing and create environments and routines that teach them how to pay attention. I wish a teacher could come live with me!

God does essentially the same with us, His children. He constantly calls us to look to Him and to listen to Him that our souls might live in abundance (John 10:10). He has given us the disciplines as means of grace to help us focus our concentration on the author and perfecter of our faith (Heb. 12:1-3). As a master teacher Himself, Jesus understood that we would need rhythms, routines, and reminders to help us learn the art of paying attention to Him. He instituted the sacraments as outward signs of inward realities, object lessons to physically remind us to focus our spiritual sight. In baptism, the washing of water refocuses our sight on the spiritual cleansing we receive through Christ; in communion, the physical bread and the wine refocus our spiritual sight on the one who died that we might be sustained. Daily intake of God's Word grabs our attention from glances at the world and refocuses our faith on the one who made the world. Regular worship with the local church similarly refocuses our attention from the chaos around and within to the Christ at the center holding all things together (Col. 1:17). Regular confession of sin forces us to admit when and how we have lost our focus while also reminding us of the forgiving, loving gaze of the Father (1 John 1:8–2:2). In these (and countless other) spiritual disciplines, God trains us in the art of paying attention.

## Anecdotes of Paying Attention

While teachers set routines and create environments, they also stir hearts through the power of story. Some of my favorite core memories feature moments when teachers read books like *Matilda* and *Bridge to Terabithia* aloud to us. As we listened, the stories and characters came alive and shaped us just as much, if not more than, the routines of the classroom. The same God who gave us the disciplines of grace knows that humans learn best through stories. In the previous chapter, we studied narratives to see the dangers of spiritual distraction. In this chapter, we will explore a few Scriptural examples of focused faith, so we can learn the art of paying attention.

When Elisha and his servant were ambushed by the army of the king of Syria in Dothan, we get a front row seat to the power of focused faith. The king of Syria, "greatly troubled" by the faith of Elisha, the prophet of Israel, sent "horses and chariots and a great army" to distract and detract him from his single-minded focus on God (2 Kings 6:11, 14). His servant was understandably fearful and taken aback when he awoke to being surrounded by an overpowering enemy army. He said, "Alas! My master! What shall we do?" to which Elisha replied, "Do not be afraid, for those who are with us are more than those who are with them" (2 Kings 6:15-16). The servant's physical gaze was set on the external circumstances, but Elisha's spiritual gaze was fully focused on his God. His focused faith engendered a bold prayer that God would open his servant's physical eyes to see the spiritual reality of which Elisha was certain. What Elisha trusted by faith, God graciously showed his servant: "So the LORD opened the eyes of the young man, and he saw, and behold, the mountain was full of horses and chariots of fire all around Elisha" (2 Kings 6:17). Elisha's servant learned a lesson that day that we must remember every day: no matter what our physical reality may be, we are invited to focus our faith on the fixed character of our faithful God.

Generations before Elisha, we find another incredible story of the power of faith focused on God. After God had emphatically rescued His people from the hand of Pharoah, one would think that their spiritual eyes would have been fixed upon Him in confidence. Yet, they had the same spiritual sight problems that we experience today. When Moses dispatched twelve choice leaders from among God's people to spy out the promised land, a living lesson about spiritual sight emerged. The twelve spies had the exact same marching orders and looked upon the exact same land and people, but they came back with very different reports. Most of the spies came back trembling with eyes fixed not on the goodness of the land but on the strength of the people who dwelled therein; however, Caleb quieted the people before Moses and said, "Let us go up at once, and occupy it, for we are well able to overcome it" (Num. 13:27-28, 30). Joshua and Caleb saw the people and the land through the lens of focused faith in God whereas the remaining spies saw through a lens of fear. Joshua sought to quiet the clamoring fears, saying, "The land which we passed through to spy it out is an exceedingly good land. If the LORD delights in us, he will bring us into this land and give it to us, a land that flows with milk and honey" (Num. 14:7-8).

God's people listened to the ten rather than the two. Consequently, they wandered for forty years. Only Caleb and Joshua survived to step into the promised land they had spied so long ago. Focused faith is no menial matter. God intends that His children learn to fix their sight on Him, not their circumstances or themselves. However, that does not mean that we are to ignore our external circumstances or our internal emotions. Faith focused on God is not a tunnel vision that ignores the realities within or without, but one that brings all such realities into His presence and under His Word. Remember, in Chapter Two, we looked at the faith of Abraham as recounted in the book of Romans. Abraham took an honest account of his body and Sarah's womb, yet "no unbelief made him waver concerning the promise of God" (Rom. 4:20). Though he was fully aware of the weakness of his body, "he grew strong in his faith as he gave glory to God, fully convinced that God was able to do what he had promised" (Rom. 4:20-21).

Faith focused on God does not mean that we lose sight of our present realities. It means that we look through our present circumstances back to God who is our ever-present help (Ps. 46:1 NIV).

## Paying Attention through Pain

Faith focused on God is not a Pollyanna, blindly optimistic faith. We do not have to ignore or deny the complexities of the situations in which we find ourselves (or the worlds which are within us) to be focused on God. God uses all our embodied lives, including our suffering and our emotions, as fodder for our faith in Him. Biblical lament plays a significant part in our spiritual sight training. Faith in God does not demand that we pretend things are easy when they are anything but. Faith in God requires that we bring our raw emotions and our real struggles into His presence, asking for His perspective, clinging to His promises.

In the same portion of Scripture where God invites us to look and listen that we might live, God tells us through the prophet Isaiah, "My thoughts are not your thoughts, neither are your ways my ways...for as the heavens are higher than the earth, so are my ways higher than your ways and my thoughts than your thoughts" (Isa. 55:8-9). When we seek to focus our attention on God through faith, we must also recognize that God works in ways that are often mysterious to us. God "knows our frame; he remembers that we are dust" (Ps. 103:14). He knows that our sight is limited even though His is the unlimited, all-knowing sight of omniscience (Prov. 15:3; Rom. 16:27). Thus, He offers us the biblical avenue of lament to bring our questions, our confusion, our anguish, and our doubt into His presence.

The minor prophet Habakkuk did not look over the grim situation of God's people with rose-colored glasses. He honestly assessed the devastation caused by Israel's lack of focused faith on God and brought his report into the presence of God. He prayed, "O Lord, I have heard the report of you, and your work, O Lord, do I fear...In wrath remember mercy" (Hab. 3:2). When the book of Habakkuk ends, the circumstances have not turned for the better. The heaviness hasn't lifted, but his eyes have. He writes a beautiful song that teaches us how to lament in faith:

> Though the fig tree should not blossom, nor fruit be on the vines, the produce of the olive fail and the fields yield no food, the flock be cut off from the fold, and there be no herd in the stalls, yet I will rejoice in the Lord; I will take joy in the God of my salvation. God, the Lord, is my strength; he makes my feet like the deer's; he makes me tread on my high places. (Hab. 3:17-19)

Through books like Job, Lamentations, and Psalms, believers are given language to express even their lack of faith in a faithful way. After all, bringing our doubts and distrust into the presence of God is the ultimate sign of faith. We show that we trust Him enough to let Him help us sort through our messy emotions, even those directed at Him.

We will explore this topic with much more depth in Chapter Seven, but for now, I simply want to be sure that we know that faith focused on God is an eyes-wide-open faith that includes all the contours of human existence even, and especially, suffering and pain. A faith concentrated on Christ has space for the honest expression of the human experience. We don't have to wrap a bow on a bone-marrow transplant or slap a smile on our face while we endure mental or physical anguish to have faith. Instead, we bring the reports of what we are seeing and experiencing into God's presence and ask for His perspective, relying on His promises and hoping in His Word.

## The Schoolhouse of Attention

Teachers train their students to cultivate attention through habits and routines and through the power of story; however, you and I both know from our experience as students that discipline is always involved. Classroom and behavior management confound me every time I substitute teach. If only it were so easy as to follow the lesson plans and properly say the prompts! But distractions abound, and students need help noticing and corralling their wandering attention.

We began this section by listening to the definition of faith set forth by the writer to the Hebrews. We will end by looking at his call to endure in our faith-training. Directly after charging the Jewish believers to fix their eyes on Jesus and to "consider him," the writer of Hebrews launches into a discourse on the loving discipline of God. He writes the following: "It is for discipline that you have to endure. God is treating you as sons.... He disciplines us for our good, that we may share in his holiness. For the moment all discipline seems painful rather than pleasant, but later it yields the peaceful fruit of righteousness to those who have been trained by it" (Heb. 12:7, 10b-11).

The writer spent an entire chapter walking the Jewish believers through a proverbial "Hall of Faith," seeking to stir their souls toward a faith focused on their God. He walks them through the hallways of historic faith to the end that they might run the race set before them with endurance, "looking to Jesus, the founder and perfecter" of their faith (Heb. 12:1-3). However, like any good teacher, he knows that learning to live with such a fixed gaze is a process that involves discipline and discomfort. He assumes that they will have to struggle against both indwelling sin and an external enemy. To use the classroom analogy, He knows that redirection and classroom management will be a vital part of their training to focus their faith on Christ.

Every Sunday, I spend sweet Sabbath time with God, confessing my sin, studying the Word, and praying for strength for the week to come. I leave my secret place with the Lord with concentrated faith on God; however, as soon as I walk through my front door, I am assaulted by a thousand pleas for my attention. The dogs need walking. The pantry needs filling. The bills need paying. My children need tending. Problems need solving. By midweek, my faith has often shifted from my Savior and settled on myself, my plans, and my strategies. Like squirmy second graders, my spiritual gaze requires constant redirection and discipline to refocus.

When the Spirit convicts us of distracted spiritual sight and wrong focal points of faith, He does so in love and faithfulness. When the Father disciplines us through the natural consequences of misplaced faith, it is proof of His fatherhood and our sonship (Heb. 12:5-6). God's children will learn their lessons, not because they are excellent students but because He is the ultimate teacher. He will complete the good work of faith He began in us (Phil. 1:6). In the new heavens and the new earth, our gazes of faith will forever be focused on Christ; in the meanwhile, we will remain in the Triune schoolhouse, learning the art of paying attention.

## Certainty & Curiosity

A faith focused on the person of Christ requires both certainty and curiosity. While initially this seems to be an odd pairing, the coupling of certainty and curiosity act like the knobs on the microscope that help us focus our attention on the only *one* who is worthy of such concentrated attention. Faith in Christ bids us be certain about the character of our God, the inerrancy of His Word, and the glories of the gospel; however, that same faith in Christ also invites us to be curious about His ways, His creation, and His people.

Once again, we find the depth of wisdom in Christ's invitation for His disciples to become like little children (Matt. 18:2-4). Children are naturally curious about the world around them, but as adults we tend to let our curiosity gather dust. It seems the worries, the cares, and the riches of the world choke out not only the seed of the gospel, but also the seeds of curiosity placed within us as humans made in the image of God (Matt. 13:22).

When my children were young, short walks to the mailbox or around the block proceeded at a snail's pace. Every stick was a sword and every leaf a treasure. A caterpillar or a puppy dog added at least twenty more minutes to the twenty-foot walk to get the mail. It took me a few years to adjust to living at the pace of their wonder. Children lean in with curiosity where adults tend to see only sameness. A quote from G.K. Chesterton regarding the "abounding vitality" and curiosity of children completely shifted my soul's posture to their pace:

> They always say, "Do it again"; and the grown-up person does it again until he is nearly dead. For grown-up people are not strong enough to exult in monotony. But perhaps God is strong enough to exult in monotony. It is possible that God says every morning, "Do it again" to the sun;

and every evening, "Do it again" to the moon. It may not be automatic necessity that makes all daisies alike; it may be that God makes every daisy separately, but has never got tired of making them. It may be that He has the eternal appetite of infancy; for we have sinned and grown old, and our Father is younger than we.[1]

If our God has "the eternal appetite of infancy," and if we are made in His image, it seems that He would delight in our curiosity toward His world and His ways. Long before microscopes, mankind looked down, up, in, and out with inquisitive eyes and awe-struck hearts. I love reading the creation accounts in the first two chapters of Genesis with a sanctified imagination. Can you imagine the giggling and laughter of Adam and Eve as they happened upon the first Okapi? If you aren't familiar with these animals, allow me to share our family's explanation of them: they look like they were created from God's "favorites" jar. They have the stripes of zebra on their hind parts, the neck of a giraffe, only shorter, and the front of a horse. When our children were young, we visited San Diego Zoo weekly for at least four years, but the Okapi exhibit never got old. Yet, the Okapi is merely one of the 1.2 million known animal species on earth. God crammed His creation with wonder. We honor the artist by giving attention to His art!

## General and Special Revelation

Theologians draw a helpful distinction between general and special revelation. General revelation refers to the things that can be learned about God by studying the created order. The apostle Paul reminds those in Rome that God's "invisible attributes, namely his eternal power and divine nature, have been clearly perceived, ever since the creation of the world, in the things that have been made" (Rom. 1:20). While general

---

1. Chesterton, G.K. *Orthodoxy*, (New York: Doubleday, 1959), 58.

revelation is available to all humans, it is insufficient for salvation. We said in a previous chapter that we need God to see God. Thus, special revelation refers to God's revelation of Himself to sinners unto salvation. The writer of Hebrews captures the concept of special revelation in the opening of his words to the Jewish believers. He reminds them that while God revealed himself "long ago, at many times and in many ways," he has spoken most clearly of himself through his Son, "whom he appointed the heir of all things, through whom he also created the world" (Heb. 1:1-2). As believers, we have received the gifts of both general and special revelation, both of which should draw our attention towards our incredibly good and gracious God.

The psalmists certainly took time to look upon creation with a curious wonder that led them to worship their God. It isn't surprising that David, who spent his formative years as a shepherd in the fields under the stars, penned a poem like Psalm 19: "The heavens declare the glory of God, and the sky above proclaims his handiwork. Day to day pours out speech, and night to night reveals knowledge. There is no speech, nor are there words, whose voice is not heard" (Ps.19:1-3).

Having wondered at creation (general revelation), he moves toward marveling at the Word of God (special revelation). Just as he extolled the glories of the galaxies, he exclaims the glories of God's words to His people:

> The law of the LORD is perfect, reviving the soul; the testimony of the LORD is sure, making wise the simple; the precepts of the LORD are right, rejoicing the heart; the commandment of the LORD is pure, enlightening the eyes; the fear of the LORD is clean, enduring forever; the rules of the LORD are true and righteous altogether. More to be desired are they than gold, even much fine gold; sweeter also than honey and the drippings of the honeycomb. (Ps. 19:7-10)

General and special revelation are meant to work in concert, as looking over God's physical world with curiosity helps us to practice cultivating attention spiritually. After all, we will better appreciate Psalm One's analogy of the godly man as a tree with deep roots if we have paid closer attention to the actual trees in our neighborhood. When God chooses to address Job's questions (special revelation), He asks a series of rhetorical questions that focus his eyes on the wonder of creation (general revelation). The nuanced detail with which God speaks of His creation shakes the dust from general revelation and stirs our souls to curious wonder. Whenever I start to lose the "abounding vitality" and "appetite of infancy" Chesterton mentioned, I spend a few hours rereading chapters 38 and 39 from the book of Job. I am left speechless every single time. Like Job, I find myself responding, "I had heard of you by the hearing of the ear, but now my eye sees you; therefore, I despise myself and repent in dust and ashes" (Job 42:5-6).

We are pendulum-hearted people; we tend to swing from one extreme to another, pulling apart what Christ intended to be wed together. No sooner do I start to revel in general revelation, than I start to neglect special revelation. Psalm 119 serves to remind us of the wonder we should have at God's revealed Word. The longest psalm in the Scriptures, this song is an elaborate poem extolling the wonders of the Word of God moving from the first to the last letters of the Hebrew alphabet. The psalmist took incredible care to create such a work. Both the work itself and the actual words therein compel us to stare a little longer at the Scriptures. He tells God, "Your testimonies are my delight; they are my counselors" (Ps. 119:24). He begs God, "Incline my heart to your testimonies, and not toward selfish gain! Turn my eyes from looking at worthless things; and give me life in your ways" (Ps. 119:36-37). He finds comfort and correction, power and protection through the Word of God (Ps. 119:50). His careful study of God's Word keeps him from sin (Ps. 119:11).

If we are serious about learning the art of cultivating attention, we do well to look with curiosity at both general and special revelation. Behind both stands the God who waits to be worshiped.

## Three Types of Curiosity

As someone who is curious by disposition, I read as many books as I can get my hands upon. Our bookshelves are overflowing and the stack of books by my bed has turned into quite a tower! I have two shelves on said bookcases that house my favorites; Ian Leslie's book *Curious* finds its home there. In my curiosity, I learned that there are three distinct types of curiosity: diversive, epistemic, and empathetic[2].

Diversive curiosity, an "attraction to everything novel," plays an important role in piquing our interest in "the new and undiscovered."[3] However, diversive curiosity has a dark side: as Leslie notes, "it can become a futile waste of energy and time, dragging us from one object of attention to another without reaping insight from any."[4] Clickbait headlines pander to our diversive curiosity. In Scripture, we find diversive curiosity used for both good and evil. Moses likely turned aside to see the bush burning yet not consumed out of diversive curiosity (Exod. 3:2-3). His curiosity about something novel enabled an encounter with the living God that shaped not only his life, but the course of Israel's history. On the other hand, we have already seen how David was drawn down a path of destruction from a sinful dart of diversive curiosity while on his roof (2 Sam. 11:2-3). When James describes the way that sin entangles us, his language of being "lured and enticed"

---

2. I explored these types of curiosity from a Christian perspective in an article for Modern Reformation (https://www.modernreformation.org/resources/articles/the-case-for-curiosity).

3. Leslie, Ian. *Curiosity: The Desire to Know and Why Your Future Depends On It*, New York: Basic Books, 2014, xx.

4. Ibid

by sinful desire smacks of diversive curiosity gone awry (James 1:14-15).

While diversive curiosity demands little of our attention, epistemic curiosity calls for concentration over time. Epistemic curiosity, a "deeper, more disciplined, and effortful" strain of curiosity, invites careful study, intentional investment, and perseverance over time.[5] Leslie notes, "epistemic curiosity can be a font of satisfaction and delight that provides sustenance for the soul."[6] The aforementioned Psalm 119 was certainly a product of epistemic curiosity, as are the great masterpieces of art and music throughout history. Moses' initial diversive curiosity toward the burning bush became a sustained curiosity about his creator. God captured Moses' glance through the burning bush, but Moses learned to cultivate a gaze of epistemic curiosity toward God throughout his life. Even at the age of 120 years old, we are told that Moses' "eye was undimmed and his vigor unabated" (Deut. 34:7). I don't think the writer referred to Moses' physical eyesight alone; rather, I believe the writer is speaking proverbially of the focused, cultivated spiritual gaze Moses had for God even in his old age. Moses did not lose his eye for "the eternal appetite of infancy." Even to the very end, he kept his sense of wonder for God. In Psalm 90 we see poetic evidence of Moses' epistemic curiosity towards His creator: "Before the mountains were brought forth, or ever you had formed the earth and the world, from everlasting to everlasting you are God" (Ps. 90:2).

Empathetic curiosity, the last of the three, expresses itself in interest "in the thoughts and feelings of other people."[7] This form of relational curiosity is as underrated as it is desperately needed in a self-seeking culture. Human beings are inherently relational creatures: we were created from Triune relationship for relationship with God and others. The Incarnate Christ

---

5. Ibid, xx, xxi.

6. Ibid, xxi.

7. Ibid, xxi.

consistently modeled empathetic curiosity. He cultivated unique relationships with each of His very different disciples, as is seen clearly in His interactions with John and Peter in the last chapter of John's Gospel (John 21:20-23). He varied His ways of interacting and communicating according to the specific needs and nuances of His audience. To some, He spoke directly, while with others He told the truth but told it slant (to use a helpful phrase by poet Emily Dickinson). Lepers and lunatics, the poor and the powerless, criminals and children, Christ met each with a careful gaze. People unaccustomed to care or the curiosity of others were astounded by His initiation toward them. The hemorrhaging woman merely wanted to touch the hem of His garment; however, Christ, sensing both her nearness and need, noticed and named her (Luke 8:43-48). She left the encounter healed in more ways than one. Christ showed similar empathetic curiosity to Zacchaeus who was hiding in a tree. After noticing and naming him, He showed empathetic interest in Zacchaeus' life by inviting Himself to dine with him (Luke 19:1-10).

In the high priestly prayer, Jesus prayed that His followers might model empathetic curiosity toward one another so that the world might know His love through ours (John 17:22-23). Underneath the New Testament's explicit "one another" commands lie an implicit invitation to empathetic curiosity (John 13:34-35; Rom. 12:10, 13: 8, 1 Pet. 1:22, among others). When small group leaders reach out during the week to check on members of their group, when a friend asks what we are learning about God, or when a parent notices the silent needs of his or her child, we practice empathetic curiosity. Such self-giving love and interest shunted outward stands out in a culture impossibly bent towards self.

Algorithms seeking to scratch our diversive curiosity abound. A glut of technology threatens to gut our attention spans. Cultivating epistemic and empathetic curiosity in such a world will take effort and intention. Thankfully, we worship a God who is infinitely interesting and worthy of our efforts to keep growing in knowledge of Him.

Thus far, we have been doing the hard yet necessary work of laying a theological foundation. We began our journey fixing our attention on the God who is attentive to us. Then, we explored the vital connection between our attention and our affections, between our looking and our love. We spent an entire chapter doing an autopsy of our distraction and inattention and then moved on to look at focused faith. With the foundation established, we will now spend our remaining time building pathways to help us practically learn how to look and listen to God that we might live!

# Part II

# Chapter Five

# The Pathway of Presence

I once listened to an entire podcast about how to breathe. Clearly, I have been breathing all my life, so, I initially rolled my eyes when a friend recommended it. But as I listened, I realized that I have been half-heartedly breathing most of my years. These poor lungs have not been pressed to their full capacity. As silly as it sounds, the process of thinking about breathing helped me breathe better. The popular placards and parcels that remind us "Just Breathe" are clearly telling us more than to remember to breathe—our brainstem does that just fine! The burgeoning phrase "Be present" belongs in the same category.

*Be present.* It seems like we shouldn't need to remind each other to do this. After all, we have no choice but to be physically present wherever we are; yet we know how hard it can be to be fully present wherever we find ourselves. Bodily, we may be at the board meeting, but mentally, we are often on the beach in Tahiti. We might be sitting in front of our desk on a Zoom call, but we all expect each other to have ten other tabs open simultaneously.

Present people, people who are truly bringing all of who they are to where they are, are a rare gift in an age of distraction. We know how it feels to bask in the presence of someone who is truly present with us. They have our gaze, and we know that we have their full attention. We know when someone is half-listening or listening-to-speak and when someone is listening-to-listen. Being fully present with others takes intention and concentration, but it begins with intention and concentration with the Lord.

Malcolm Muggeridge had the tall task of writing a biography of Mother Theresa, someone whom people described as incredibly present. In assessing the task before him, he noted, "The wholly dedicated like Mother Theresa do not have biographies. Biographically speaking, nothing happens to them. To live for, and in, others… is to eliminate happenings, which are a factor of the ego and the will."[1] He continued, "She gave herself to Christ and through him to her neighbor. This was the end of her biography and the beginning of her life."[2]

When we are preoccupied with self and the stuff of biography, to use Muggeridge's phraseology, we cannot be fully present. Present people are free to be with others completely because they continually entrust their lives to God.

## Preoccupation and Presence

The human heart weighs less than a pound and the human brain less than three, yet both carry much more "weight". Our lives are cumbered with cares, and our minds are weighed down by worries. We are finite creatures with limited capacities. We are dignified derivatives: *dignified* in that we have been made uniquely in the image of God, *derivative* in that we have no life on our own. Every breath we breathe is bequeathed to us, every ability we have comes from the self-existing, eternal God who created us. It does not take much for us to become flooded and preoccupied.

---

1. Muggeridge, Malcolm. *Something Beautiful for God* (New York: Ballantine Books, 1971), 4.

2. Ibid, 4.

Preoccupied means to be so engrossed with thoughts of something or someone that you are unable to engage in other things; it comes from the Latin *praeoccupare* which literally means to "seize beforehand." When my heart and mind are already occupied with other things, there is no space for being present to others, primarily God Himself.

Sure, I may be bodily present; however, in a state of preoccupation my soul is not spacious enough for the people that God places in front of me, be they my children, neighbors, or strangers. In a worried, frenetic, preoccupied state, souls have all the welcome of a pin cushion, according to Henri Nouwen.[3]

Although we are often surprised by our limitations, God isn't. He created us to live in delighted dependence upon Him. He intended that we would trust Him to provide all we needed. His infinitude is a perfect pairing for our finiteness, His abundance a perfect partner for our neediness. Those who have been restored to a right relationship with God through Christ don't have to live preoccupied with their own cares. In the Sermon on the Mount, after He bids His disciples to look at the birds and to consider the lilies, He speaks directly, saying the following:

> Therefore, do not be anxious, saying, 'What shall we eat?' or 'What shall we drink?' or 'What shall we wear?' For the Gentiles seek after all these things, and your heavenly Father knows that you need them all. But seek first the kingdom of God and his righteousness, and all these things will be added to you. (Matt. 6:31-33)

Jesus knew the human tendency to be preoccupied with our basic needs; however, He wanted His disciples to see that God's care for them frees them to seek after higher things. The disciples, who spent considerable time listening to Jesus'

---

3. Nouwen, Henri. *The Genesee Diary: Report from a Trappist Monastery.* (New York: Doubleday, 1976), 145.

sermons and watching His life, passed along similar lessons to their disciples. The apostle Paul reminded the Philippians, "Do not be anxious about anything, but in everything by prayer and supplication with thanksgiving let your requests be made known to God. And the peace of God, which surpasses all understanding will guard your hearts and your minds in Christ Jesus" (Phil. 4:6-7). The apostle Peter told church leaders, encumbered by the cares of their flocks, "Humble yourselves.... casting all your anxieties on him, because he cares for you" (1 Pet. 5:6; 7).

Those who know that the unlimited, all-powerful, all-wise God of the universe actively cares for them are freed from selfish preoccupation to become more present people. Simone Weil wrote, "It is not my business to think about myself. My business is to think about God. It is for God to think about me."[4]

These commands may be simple, but they are far from easy to practice. As someone who tends towards anxiety, the act of casting cares upon the Lord feels like a constant conveyor belt or an old-fashioned game of Hot Potato. As soon as one care leaves, another worry shows up. It takes great effort and requires great trust to bring the needs of each day to the Lord every morning, believing He cares more than I do. Yet, those who have spent time in the presence of the Lord are freed to be present with others. Casting off preoccupations creates space and presence which are rare commodities in our crowded lives. We remember that we are loved people freed to love people.

## The Significance of Place

In addition to being less preoccupied with self, we must learn the significance of place if we seek to become more present people. Earlier we mentioned our innate limitations as humans. We have limited mental, emotional, and relational capacities.

---

4. Weil, 50-51.

As obvious as it may seem, it is significant to note our physical limitations. As embodied creatures who live within the constraints of time and space, we can physically only be in one place at one time. Every time I sit in a plane, I stare out the window in wonder of the reality of being shuttled through the air. Science and technology are incredible tools, but they cannot allow us to be in two places at once.

While there are countless benefits afforded to us in a world flattened through globalization and technology, Neil Postman warned us of the potential dangers. When the world is literally in our palms, we sometimes lose our sense of place. As those who process five times more information a day than our counterparts did in the 1980s, we are more likely to feel powerless and placeless.[5] Postman introduced me to the idea of action-value, which I've found helpful in landing me back in the local in a global world. He explains that "information derives its importance from the possibilities of action." He continues, "Prior to the age of telegraphy, the information-action ratio was sufficiently close so that most people had a sense of being able to control some of the contingencies in their lives. What people knew had action-value."[6]

Much of the information we receive comes from other continents. We know things happening in real time that have no actual action-value in our lives. We see images of wars that we can do nothing to change as we read tweets about the personal details of the lives of people whom we don't even know. No wonder we feel lost in the glut of globalized information. As Postman concluded, "Most of our daily news is inert, consisting of information that gives us something to talk about but cannot lead to meaningful action."[7] We were never intended to process so much information. As Daniel

---

5. Levitin, 6.

6. Postman, Neil. *Amusing Ourselves to Death: Public Discourse in the Age of Show Business*, (New York: Penguin Books, 1986), 69.

7. Ibid, 68.

Levitin explains, there is an "informational speed limit" (about 120 bits per second) which limits us to being able to understand only two to three people talking at a time. He writes, "We're surrounded on this planet by billions of other humans, but we can understand only two at a time at the most!"[8] Levitin, who is not coming from the Christian worldview, understands that "attention is the most essential mental resource for any organism."[9]

Attention is a limited resource. We were made to be bodily present in the places the Lord has allotted for us. When we spend too much time reading about what is happening in the world, it robs us of attention intended to be used in the places God has placed us. We will become more present people when we learn to limit the amount of information we process to actual action-value. We can't support every cause, but we can choose to support a local cause that blesses the people whom God has placed around us as neighbors. We cannot control who is elected as a ruler in a foreign election, but we can actively engage in local politics or serve through civic organizations in our area. The more we seek to engage in the places closest to us and invest in the people nearest to us, the more we will be freed to be present in a globalized world.

When the apostle Paul stood amid the Areopagus, he addressed the people of Athens saying, "And he made from one man every nation of mankind to live on all the face of the earth, having determined allotted periods and the boundaries of their dwelling place, that they should seek God" (Acts 17:26-27). We are a people who know not only where we live, but also the God who has chosen us to live there for great purpose.

In a globalized world, active involvement in the local church plays a deeply significant role. Even though we have access to thousands upon thousands of sermons, the local church provides shepherds and elders with local and personal

---

8. Levitin, 7.
9. Ibid.

knowledge of their flocks. The Great Commission is to be lived out within local congregations who are seeking to share the gospel in their specific neighborhoods with their neighbors (Matt. 28:18-20). Our mission has a global scope but is lived out of a local focus.

## Restlessness and Rest

The French diplomat Alexis de Tocqueville visited America shortly after its founding with a heart full of curiosity to study our nascent democracy. He left no part of American life or society unturned and recorded his keen observations in a thick book called *Democracy in America*. Much of what he wrote hundreds of years ago feels like it could have been written twenty years ago, not least his thoughts on the spirit of restlessness and rootlessness in American society:

> In the United States a man builds a house in which to spend his old age, and he sells it before the roof is on; he plants a garden and lets it just as the trees are coming into bearing; he brings a field into tillage and leaves other men to gather the crops; he embraces a profession and gives it up; he settles in a place which he soon afterwards leaves to carry his changeable longings elsewhere...At first sight there is something surprising in this strange unrest of so many happy men, restless in the midst of abundance. The spectacle itself, however, is as old as the world; the novelty is to see a whole people furnish an exemplification of it.[10]

Long before social media newsfeeds fed our wanderlust to be "anywhere but here," de Tocqueville remarked on the uniqueness of a whole people "restless in the midst of abundance." Despite all the mind-boggling abundance surrounding us, we struggle to be present and to stay where we are. We move about much

---

10. Alexis de Tocqueville, *Democracy in America*, (New York: Bantam Books, 2004), 659-659.

– whether physically chasing greener pastures or mentally doing so in our daydreams. The internet did not create our sin struggles of discontentment, though it most certainly exacerbated them. God's people showed a similar penchant for restlessness before the first smartphone or the founding of the United States. God spoke strong words concerning Israel's restlessness through the prophet Jeremiah: "How much you go about changing your way! You shall be put to shame by Egypt as you were put to shame by Assyria" (Jer. 2:36).

When circumstances grew hard, God's people quickly sought to change them. They continually looked to other people and places when God wanted them to trust His provision and His plans for them. Over *there* looked better than right *here*, a sentiment we share thousands of years later. God pleaded with His people to live within the lots He assigned for them and to look to Him for life. He reminded them to lift their eyes from circumstances to their source!

Both King David and Asaph struggled with peering at the lots of others and longing for their circumstances rather than the lot God assigned him. The entire first half of Psalm 73 records Asaph's restless, jealous feelings as he looks at the apparent ease of the evildoers all around him. However, when he enters the Temple, God grabs his gaze and fixes his attention back where it belongs: on the nearness of his God. Asaph moves from restlessness to rest, from wanting to be everywhere else to being present with his God: "But as for me it is good to be near God; I have made the Lord God my refuge, that I may tell of all your works" (Ps. 73:28). David expresses a similar juxtaposition of restlessness and rest. David notes, "The sorrows of those who run after another god shall multiply" (Ps. 16:4). He reminds himself that pleasure is found in the presence of the Lord, saying, "You make known to me the path of life; in your presence there is fullness of joy; at your right hand are pleasures forevermore" (Ps. 16:11). Restlessness becomes rest when we begin to live within our lots. David's words still settle souls:

"The LORD is my chosen portion and my cup; you hold my lot. The lines have fallen for me in pleasant places; indeed, I have a beautiful inheritance (Ps. 16:5-6).

It takes great power to live present lives in an age marked by restlessness. Our phones offer endless invitations to peer into others' lots which often stirs up a spirit of restlessness and discontentment. We learn to live within our lots when we remember what Elisabeth Elliot wisely wrote: "The secret is Christ in me, not a different set of circumstances."[11] When prison was the Lord's lot for Paul, he was able to say, "I have learned in whatever situation I am to be content.... I can do all things through him who strengthens me" (Phil. 4:11, 13). The same God who draws our lot strengthens us to live within it. Our present God empowers us to be present right where He has us. As one who struggles to be joyfully present within my lot, I pray, "Lord, help me to be where my feet are."

## Loving Locally

In *The Screwtape Letters*, C.S. Lewis depicts a novice demon learning the art of tempting and sidelining a new convert to Christianity. The letters back and forth between the more experienced demon, Screwtape, and his protégé, Wormwood, both entertain and convict thoughtful readers. Noting the coexistence of both benevolence and malevolence in the new convert's soul, Screwtape offers Wormwood the following advice:

> But, do what you will, there is going to be some benevolence, as well as some malice, in your patient's soul. The great thing is to direct the malice to his immediate neighbours whom he meets every day and to thrust his benevolence out to the remote circumference,

---

11. Elliot, Elisabeth. *Keep a Quiet Heart*, (Grand Rapids: Revell, 1995), 20.

to people he does not know. The malice thus becomes wholly real and the benevolence largely imaginary.[12]

Wormwood's sage advice is to push all the "patient's" feelings of love and goodwill toward broad generalities while pushing all the ill will towards the specific people in his daily life. The Enemy seems to employ this tactic today as well. I see yard placards all over our city saying "Humankind: Be human. Be kind." Clothing stores are making a pretty penny selling shirts with similar mottos. People love the idea of loving each other, in theory; however, we struggle in practice with the real people who surround us. As the hymn writer Frances Ridley Havergal noted, "When we take a wide sweep, we are so apt to be vague. When we are aiming at generalities, we do not hit the practicalities."[13]

The Scriptures heartily agree with the sign placards, but they expect us to practice them through the power of the Holy Spirit. Jesus wasn't throwing out pithy statements when He told us to love our neighbor as ourselves and to love our enemies— He intended that we learn to live with such supernatural love (Matt. 5:43-48, 22:37-40). Jesus modeled such love for us, in that while we were still His enemies willfully sinning against Him, Christ died for us (Rom. 5:7-10). Those who have received such forgiveness and love are expected to offer it freely to others. As Jesus told the disciples who were gawking at the sinful woman who washed His feet with her tears and dried them with her hair, those who are forgiven much love much (Luke 7:44-47).

I had a chance to practice loving locally even as I was writing this chapter. The words were flowing, but my youngest son came into my room with a fever. It would have been much easier to keep waxing eloquent about being present with those who live within our lots, but the Spirit prompted me to close my computer and pay attention to my son. I cannot make his

---

12. Lewis, C.S. *The Screwtape Letters*, (Old Tappan: Revell, 1976), 43.
13. Havergal, Frances Ridley. *Kept for the Master's Use*, (Chicago: Moody), 25.

fever go away, but I can offer him the gift of focused presence and attention. Loving locally implies that we begin to embrace our limitations, recognizing that we cannot always be all things to all people. Every "yes" we offer to be present with someone presumes many "nos." As we schedule our weeks and mete out our moments, we need to be walking with the Spirit and seeking to live within our God-given priorities. As my husband reminds me weekly, "Do what only you can do." Many people can write articles on loving locally, but no one else can care for my sickly son.

In her hymn, "Father, I Know that All My Life," Anna Waring wrote multiple stanzas that have become my consistent prayer.

"I ask thee for a thoughtful love, through constant watching wise
To meet the glad with joyful smiles, and to wipe the weeping eyes;
And a heart at leisure from itself, to soothe and sympathize.

I would not have the restless will that hurries to and fro,
Seeking for some great thing to do or secret thing to know;
I would be treated as a child, and guided where I go.

Wherever in the world I am, in whatso'er estate,
I have a fellowship with hearts to keep and cultivate;
And a work of lowly love to do for the Lord on whom I wait."[14]

## Attunement and Presence

One of the ways I have sought to love the locals who live within my home is to approach parenting as my profession. Just as my nurse friends have yearly requirements for ongoing education, my husband and I have sought to make a syllabus

---

14. https://www.hymnal.net/en/hymn/ns/12

for our own continuing education as parents. In the past five years, I learned a new word and accompanying concept that have radically changed the way I seek to be present to God, to my children, and to the other locals in my life: attunement.

Attunement is the reactiveness we have to another person; it describes the process by which we form relationships. Using the language we learned in the previous chapter about the three types of curiosity, attuning to others is a way to practice empathetic curiosity. Dr. Dan Siegel writes the following concerning attunement:

> When we attune with others we allow our own internal state to shift, to come to resonate with the inner world of another. This resonance is at the heart of the important sense of 'feeling felt' that emerges in close relationships. Children need attunement to feel secure and to develop well, and throughout our lives we need attunement to feel close and connected.[15]

We practice attunement when we notice our child's body language or wonder about his hefty sigh during homework. We practice attunement when we ask questions with a gentle, caring cadence. We practice attunement when we soothe a scared child rather than shaming her. We practice attunement when we stack our phones on the counter so that we can fully engage with our eyes and our heart over family dinner. At base, attunement is attention.

The scary news is that while so much depends on loving attention, the world, the flesh, and the devil are constantly seeking to distract us. Curt Thompson wrote the following: "In the age of the internet we are learning—in fact we are practicing—how to not pay attention. We are being trained to be unable to maintain attunement to a whole host of things

---

15. Siegel, Dan. *Mindsight: The New Science of Personal Transformation*, (New York: Bantam, 2011), 27.

whose flourishing depends on our paying attention for extended periods of time."[16]

Attunement is a significant factor in children creating healthy attachments in their formative years. Children create relational habits out of their experiences with their caregivers which they carry into adulthood. But attunement is not simply for parents and children: a pastor can be attuned to his flock, a spouse to his or her partner, and a friend to another friend. In fact, those who grew up without the priceless gift of a healthy attachment grow and heal in adulthood through such loving, attentive care. Things broken in family need to be healed in family, and the church is a family by better blood.

Experts say that even the most observant parents will only track with their children 45 to 50 percent of the time. So, batting 400 is winning, even if it feels like you are losing. We do our best as broken vessels with limited access to the secret places of the heart. Thankfully, as Curt Thompson says, "God does not expect parents to be perfect. He does, however, long for us to be perceptive."[17]

Being attuned to our boys and their emotional needs as teenagers feels like it has been my full-time job of late: noticing their body cues, asking them questions, providing a nurturing place to process and a net upon which to fall. These are the privileges of being a parent, but I feel wildly unqualified for this job.

## The God of Attunement

The incredible news for us as we seek to be attuned to others is that attunement neither starts nor ends with us. The God who wired the human for attachment and set up our souls for connection did so because He is an attuned God. God has

---

16. Thompson, Curt. *The Soul of Desire: Discovering the Neuroscience of Longing, Beauty, and Community*, (Downers Grove: IVP, 2021), 146.

17. Thompson, Curt. *The Anatomy of the Soul*, (Carol Stream: Tyndale Momentum, 2010), 121.

attached Himself to His people through His covenant love. It is evident that the unearned, unconditional love of God which we have received by grace through faith changes us from the inside out. We have already looked at Deuteronomy where God tells His people that He set His love on them, He chose them (Deut. 7:6-9, 9:6-8). Once cemented through the covenants, God's attention has been set on His people. Through the prophet Hosea, we hear God use similar language of attached love for His people:

> When Israel was a child, I loved him, and out of Egypt I called my son. The more they were called, the more they went away…Yet it is I who taught Ephraim to walk; I took them up by their arms, but they did not know that I healed them. I led them with cords of kindness and with bands of love, and I became to them as one who eases the yoke on their jaws, and I bent down to them and fed them. (Hosea 11:1-4)

Despite their sinful lack of attention to their God, God refuses to break his covenant. He remains attuned to them. His heart breaks out in deeply attached covenant love, saying, "How can I give you up, O Ephraim? How can I hand you over, O Israel?... My heart recoils within me; my compassion grows warm and tender; I will not execute my burning anger; I will not again destroy Ephraim; for I am God and not a man, the Holy One in your midst, and I will not come in wrath" (Hos. 11:8-9).

We know what Hosea didn't. The Holy God would pour out the cup of His wrath not on we who earned it, but on His perfect Son (Isa. 51:22; Matt. 20:22). He kept His covenant with us through the cross of Christ. God the Father turned His face away from His always attentive Son so that He might turn His gaze towards us. Through Christ, we now have unparalleled access to our God who is attuned to us! We will not be able to be attuned to others unless we are shaped by the love of our attentive and attuned God.

## Watching Him Watching Us

My son aspires to be a sports journalist, so, from time to time, he borrows my computer to type up his latest news story. On one such day, when he came into my room, he didn't notice that I was sitting on my bed reading. He simply put on his dad's headphones and happily typed to his heart's content, unaware of my presence with him. As I sat there, watching him do what he loves, tears pooled in my eyes.

Writing can be a lonely calling, and I had been struggling with insecurity and fears as a writer that month. As I sat with my heart nearly bursting from parental pride watching my son write, I sensed God's nearness to me. I realized that when I sit at my desk to work on writing, I am never alone. God is with me, watching with interest and care, as I was with my son. A single moment of attunement to God shaped me profoundly.

The awareness of God's attention is a powerful shaping force. As the apostle Paul contended to the Church in Rome, "What then shall we say to these things? If God is for us, who can be against us?" (Rom. 8:31). When we realize that absolutely nothing can separate us from the love of God, we become a deeply courageous people (Rom. 8:35-39). David understood that when we begin to grasp that there is no place where God is not attuned to us, we cannot help but be transformed by His attentive care: "Where shall I go from your Spirit? Or where shall I flee from your presence? If I ascend to heaven, you are there! If I make my bed in Sheol, you are there! If I take the wings of the morning and dwell in the uttermost parts of the sea, even there your hand shall lead me, and your right hand shall hold me" (Ps. 139:7-10).

The more we begin to enjoy the presence of God, the sooner we will be transformed into more present people. When we understand that the omniscient, omnipresent God of the universe occupies Himself with thoughts of us, we will become less preoccupied with ourselves and more available and attentive to the people around us (Ps. 139:17-18). The better we trust the God who has allotted our present portions and drawn up our specific lots, the more present we will be in our respective places. Having explored the pathway of presence as one way to cultivate attention in a distracting world, we will now move on to the pathway of beauty!

# Chapter Six

# The Pathway of Beauty

Try as I may to encourage a love for the classics in my progeny, my teenagers persist in loving dystopic novels instead. I joke with them that all dystopic novels are the same (to which they might rightly reply that the same could be said of Jane Austen's novels). In the countless hours I have spent reading them aloud or listening to them, I have learned that most dystopic novels feature a cold, utilitarian society in which the arts and creativity have been forbidden. Yet, somehow, the deeply human longing for beauty, love, and hope always emerges.

We drive for days across the country to see National Parks because we hunger for beauty. We stand in lines overnight to get tickets to a concert because we hunger for beauty. We stay up into the wee hours of the morning to finish the novel because we hunger for beauty. Humans are wired for beauty because we were created in the image of a beautiful God. We long to express innate creativity because we were made in the image of the creator of all things. Sin may dull such desires and harden our hearts, but deep within us, we know beauty when we see it.

## Our Beautiful God

Thankfully, our God did not create a dystopic, utilitarian world. He created the colorful, varied, nuanced globe on which we live. He set it spinning at the exact right speed to enable human flourishing. He set our planet in the "Goldilocks Zone," the only location in space that allows human beings to exist safely. If we were any closer to the sun, we would burn up, any further, we would freeze. He engineered the unique properties of water (polarity, high heat capacity, cohesion, adhesion, etc.) so that humanity could thrive. Clearly, our God is an excellent scientist and engineer, but He is also an incredible artist.

The first time we meet God, He is an artist in His studio creating the world *ex nihilo* (out of nothing) with the power of His creative word (Gen. 1–2). He simply speaks and things are. He created the elephant, the giraffe, and the creatures who live in the Mariana Trench with mere syllables. He made evergreens and cypresses and water lilies with a word. As we have already established in Chapter Four, creation itself teaches us something about the nature and power of our God. However, if we stop short of the Spirit-empowered work of climbing back up the sunbeams to the sun, we'll find ourselves slipping into idolatry. As Paul said in the beginning of his words to the church at Rome, when we worship and serve created things rather than the creator, we become "futile in our thinking" with darkened, foolish hearts (Rom. 1:21-23). The beauty of creation should always lead us back to our beautiful God.

In addition to creation, God's interactions with His people also show us that our God cares about beauty. At the founding of Israel, God gave Moses elaborate instructions regarding the construction of the Ark of the Covenant (a provisional solution for a holy God to dwell among His unholy people). Anyone who has ever sought to read the Bible in a year knows the incredible amount of intricate detail God gives to Moses regarding a temporary tent. God gives a detailed supply list, exact measurements, and an oral outline for the sculpting of golden angels (Exod. 25). The tables, the curtains, the lampstands, the clothing of the priests: all are spelled out in intricate detail and contain fine artistic elements like hammered almond blossoms and precious stone inlays and embroidered pomegranates (Exod. 26-28). Not only are these artistic instructions mentioned once, but they are also repeated as they are fulfilled (much like a "To Do" list and a "Done" list).

God doesn't simply give instructions; His very Spirit empowers all the creative work (Exod. 31:3). The Spirit of God filled the artists "with ability and intelligence, with knowledge and all craftsmanship, to devise artistic designs, to work in gold, silver, and bronze" (Exod. 31:3-4). God is both an artist and a creator of other artists!

When Jesus was on the earth, He drew the eyes of His disciples toward natural and human beauty. He enjoyed good food and good company, so much so that many accused Him of a being a glutton and drunkard (Matt. 11:19). His first miracle took place at a wedding party where He turned water into wine so that the family of the couple would not be ashamed and the beautiful evening could continue (John 2:1-12).

The things of the earth matter, but they only matter in so far as they turn our gaze back to the one who stands behind it all! While he was exiled on the island of Patmos, God gave the apostle John a vision of the city and the life to come after Jesus' second coming. In what sounds like the detailed instructions God gave Moses, we hear about the holy city, the New Jerusalem, which will feature high walls (security) with foundations of jewels (beauty). A river will flow through the city (beauty) and a massive tree bearing twelve kinds of fruits will grow there (Rev. 21: 9–22:5). As beautiful as it all sounds, let us not miss the most beautiful part: the Lamb at the center of the throne (Rev. 7:9-10). We will spend eternal days in the new heavens and the new earth falling in awe before our beautiful God (Rev. 22:1-5). Our days on this beautiful, but broken spinning globe offer countless opportunities for us to practice doing now what we will do for all eternity.

## The Language of Longing

As a writer, I am quite comfortable in the world of words. I feel great security in libraries and bookstores which are refuges for me. However, for the past few years, I have been learning the language of longing—which feels very uncomfortable for me. As a type-A person, I love efficiency and solutions, but as I am raising teenagers and getting more comfortable in my own skin, I have had to learn to become more comfortable in the world of longings and desires. Underneath our actual words are whole worlds of nearly unutterable longings—longings for beauty, significance, safety, and love. Long before I stumbled into the language of human longing, C.S. Lewis wrote the following about it:

> In speaking of this desire for our own far-off country, which we find in ourselves even now, I feel a certain shyness. I am almost committing an indecency. I am trying to rip open the inconsolable secret in each one of you—the secret which hurts so much that you take revenge on it by calling it names like Nostalgia and Romanticism and Adolescence...The books or the music in which we thought the beauty was located will betray us if we trust them; it was not in them, it only came through them, and what came through them was longing....For they are not the thing itself; they are only the scent of a flower we have not found, the echo of a tune we have not heard, news from a country we have never yet visited.[1]

Lewis' words resonate deeply with us because God has set eternity within us (Eccles. 3:11). We were never made only for this world; we were created out of the depth of love within the

---

1. Lewis, C.S. *The Weight of Glory*, (San Francisco: Harper, 1976), 30-31.

Trinity. We were made to be face-to-face with the beautiful God who authors every atom and sketches every sunset. In a fallen and badly broken world, our longings are intended to be homing devices that reorient us to the eternal life for which we were created. St. Augustine wrote, "The whole life of the good Christian is a holy longing."[2]

It is difficult and uncomfortable to live with the tension of longing; many of us much prefer to deaden our desires and lower our expectations. Others demand that their desires be satisfied here and now, and thus become enslaved to longings and desires. Believers understand that we are neither to efface our longings nor enthrone them; rather, we are invited to continually entrust them to the one who created both us and them. Our longings, both met and unmet, are intended to lead us all the way home to the presence of the only one who can satisfy them. In the words of Andrew MacLaren, "The secret of all our unrest is the going out of our desires after earthly things…The secret of satisfied repose is to set our affections thoroughly on God."[3]

## Created to Create

In a culture where everyone claims to be experts, we have lost the beauty of amateurs. Typically, we think of amateurs as beginners or novices, green and naïve as compared to their skilled, paid counterparts; however, the word "amateur" comes from the Latin *amatore* and literally means "one who loves." We may not have the musical ear of Bach or the painting prowess of Van Gogh, but we are each created in the image of a creative God. Thus, we are innately wired to image God by creating. As amateurs, we are free to love God in and through the act of creating!

---

2. Saint Augustine, *Later Works*, ed. John Burnaby, (Philadelphia: Westminster John Knox, 1995), 290.

3. MacLaren, Andrew. "Man's True Treasure in God" (https://biblehub.com/commentaries/maclaren/psalms/16.htm)

We don't have to be prodigies or meet certain proficiencies to create. If my house were ever to catch on fire, before I grabbed any other nonliving thing, I would grab a basket that sits in my bedside table which overflows with my children's art and writing over the years. I treasure those tidbits of silly sketches and clumsy poetry more than most things on earth. I love them because I love the ones who made them. Their efforts which reveal their hearts hold endless value to me. The Lord feels the same way about our attempts at imaging Him as a creator. He loves them because He loves us. He enjoys the process we engage in with Him as much as the product itself.

In an Amazon world full of consumption, any act of creativity helps check the rising tide of consumerism. James K.A. Smith wittily describes how deeply consumerism insidiously shapes us: "'What is the chief end of man?' The consumerist catechism asks. 'To acquire stuff with the illusion that I can enjoy it forever'."[4]

The Westminster Shorter Catechism's actual answer is "To glorify God and enjoy him forever."[5] Joining God as little co-creators is certainly one way to practice it! Once again, we find ourselves back to the wisdom laced in Jesus' statement that we ought to have faith like children. Children are consummate creators. They never tire of creating; they don't let the silent vetoes of adulthood stop them from setting out to make something new. We have so much to learn from children, especially when it comes to being creative. Madeline L'Engle advises artists similarly, saying, "We cannot be mature artists if we have lost the ability to believe which we had as children."[6]

Creativity channels and focuses our attention, requiring our concentration and presence. It frees us from the choking

---

4. James K. A. Smith, *You are What You Love,* (Grand Rapids: Brazos Press, 2016), 86.

5. Williamson, G.I. *The Westminster Confession of Faith for Study Classes.* (Philadelphia: Presbyterian and Reformed, 1964), 46.

6. L'Engle, Madeline. *Walking on Water: Reflections on Faith & Art,* (New York: Convergent Books, 1980), 47.

love of self and becomes a shared lane between us and our creator God. Creativity comes in many forms, but for the sake of space, we will briefly explore a few.

## Art

I thought I knew the famous painting 'American Gothic' by Grant Wood, until I read an entire book about the painting. That's right—an entire book about one painting. Apparently, learning to look is an art that takes practice and precision. In a culture where books are written about speed-reading, slowing down to truly see and savor the beauty of art is an underrated habit. We move so quickly that it takes work to linger long before a painting to truly observe and see the work set before us.

Dr. Curt Thompson, a believing psychiatrist, asks his clients to do a strange thing when he begins to meet with them: he invites them to spend time each day contemplating a work of art. His clients are understandably dubious; after all, they come to him desperate for help with addictions, failing marriages, and difficult relationships with their children. They don't see how art has anything to offer them. However, Thompson has learned to bring the power of art into his practice. Art awakens longing, and most of our pain starts at the level of longing.[7]

Viewing art is meant to be a two-sided experience. We are not to passively sit and watch, but to actively engage in the work set before us. As Madeline L'Engle, the author of *A Wrinkle in Time*, explains, "Art should communicate with as many people as possible, not just with a group of the esoteric elite."[8] Here again, we need not let expertise (or lack thereof) rob us of the experience offered to us through the visual arts. We don't need to travel to the Louvre to enjoy God through the appreciation of art. We don't need passports to be participants

---

7. Thompson, Curt. *The Soul of Desire: Discovering the Neuroscience of Longing, Beauty, and Community*, (Downers Grove: IVP, 2021), 3-5.

8. L'Engle, 42.

in the beauty of art. We can check out books at the library, watch documentaries about artists, or visit local art exhibits without even leaving our localities.

When we engage in the visual arts as believers, we can ask some of the following questions to help look *through* the beauty back *to* the beautiful God:

- To what are my eyes first drawn in this work? Why do I think that is so?
- What longings does this painting stir within me?
- Does this work show off creation, the fall, redemption, or future glory? If so, how?

## Nature

Since the Covid pandemic, the National Parks service has reported a marked spike in visitors (an over 25 percent increase). Something about being shut up in rooms under electric lights for over a year stirred a hunger in us for the glories of the outdoors! It is difficult to think of your ego when you are standing in front of the Pacific Ocean or atop the Grand Canyon (though selfies certainly regularly re-insert the self). We go to beautiful places and hike hard trails because, somewhere deep within us, we need to feel small and to experience what C.S. Lewis calls the "pleasure of the inferior." Lewis notes "the pleasure of a beast before men, a child before its father, a pupil before his teacher, a creature before its Creator."[9] Even in a self-obsessed world, we hunger for even proximate experiences of the unique pleasure of the inferior. Through the natural world, God, in His common grace, offers His creatures a proper sense of proportion. Something about walking in the shade of massive Redwood trees that have been on the earth for thousands of years reminds us of our smallness.

God intends natural beauty to lead His children to supernatural worship! This is the difference between common

---

9. Lewis, C.S. *The Weight of Glory*, 37.

grace and special grace, general revelation and special revelation. Only by the help of the Holy Spirit can we fully climb back up the sunbeam to the sun, as we discussed in Chapter Four. We see such a progression throughout the psalms but most notably in Psalm 8. David bookends this song of praise to God with the same phrase: "O LORD, our God, how majestic is your name in all the earth!" (Ps. 8:1, 9). In the middle of the psalm, we learn what led him to such heights of worship: "When I look at your heavens, the work of your fingers, the moon and the stars, which you have set in place, what is man that you are mindful of him, and the son of man that you care for him?" (Ps. 8:3-4). David's careful considering of the natural world lifted his heart into supernatural praise for its creator.

Once again, I invite us into the joy of the amateur. We don't need to have a PhD in Biology to appreciate the flora and fauna of our respective climates. We don't have to understand complex math equations to marvel at the images captured by the Hubble Space Telescope. One small thing I've built into my daily schedule is a short "wonder walk." During these ten-minute sessions, I simply walk through my neighborhood with eyes looking attentively for small avenues through which to worship God! It may be the dappled colors of the rose up the street or the gentle breeze that grab my gaze and lift it upwards! Sometimes I thank God for His consistency in causing the same sun to rise every morning. Other times I grapple with the reality that gravity holds my feet firmly on the ground as the globe spins at approximately a thousand miles an hour! The key is not stopping short where our flesh would halt us. We must move beyond and behind the created order to the glorious creator who spoke it - and us - into existence.

## Poetry

"Water, water, everywhere, nor any drop to drink," wrote Samuel Taylor Coleridge in *The Rime of the Ancient Mariner*. While I can't relate to the irony of a sailor feeling parched when surrounded by water, the phrase captures how I feel about words in our present age. We live in a society and an era where words are ubiquitous, yet so often I find myself starving for life-giving, deeply significant words.

Advertisements and billboards constantly bombard us with words. With the internet, we have access to more books and publications than ever before; however, the inundation of words, many of them empty, can easily overwhelm us. In a fast-moving, loquacious society, poetry, with its economy of words, teaches us to slow down and savor words with deep and double meanings. Poetry, speaking in the language of longing, does a deep work in the human soul, taking us to places that epistles and narratives often do not. Though concise and tight in form, poetry offers expansive places for souls. As such, we ought not to be surprised that poetry comprises about one-third of the Scriptures. Although there are a handful of books in the Bible which are considered poetry (Psalms, Proverbs, Song of Solomon, Job, and Ecclesiastes), bits and pieces of poetry are laced throughout the entire canon.

In addition to the poetry offered within the Scriptures themselves, believers have inherited a long lineage of devotional poetry. Even though I was a literature major in college, I did not discover the depth of devotional poetry until my late twenties. When I did, it was as if a whole new world was opened to me. Through poets like St. John of the Cross, George Herbert, Christina Rosetti, George MacDonald, and Luci Shaw, I found kindred spirits across the generations of the Christian faith. They help me to see and savor God through the eyes and language of another, bringing light and putting words to "the inconsolable secret" C.S. Lewis mentioned.

Sunday by Sunday, when we rise to take communion at church, I meditate on Herbert's beautiful stanza,

"Love is that liquor sweet and most divine
which my God feels as blood; but I, as wine."[10]

---

10. Herbert, George. "The Agony," *The Country Parson, The Temple*, (New York: Paulist Press, 1981), 151.

When my ego starts to demand praise and adulation from man, I remember a short line from George MacDonald that points me back to the audience of one:

> "'Tis God I need, not rank in God
> 'Tis life, not honor's mead
> With him to fill my every mood
> I am content, indeed."[11]

When suffering hits and takes my breath away, I pull out my tattered collection of Christina Rossetti poems and thumb until I find the following favorite lines:

> "Christ's Heart was wrung for me, if mine is sore
> And if my feet are weary, His have bled
> He had no place wherein to lay His head;
> If I am burdened, He was burdened more,
> The cup I drink, He drank of long before."[12]

For those who haven't had the privilege of exposure to poetry, the psalms are an excellent (and God-breathed) place to start seeing and savoring God outside of prose. Additionally, anthologies of sacramental poems throughout history provide introductions to various styles and voices within poetry.[13]

## Music

I am admittedly tone-deaf and mostly musically illiterate, but I will take my own advice and lean into being an amateur when it comes to enjoying God through music. After all, the psalms are replete with commands to grab an instrument with which to make joyful music to our God. We are commanded,

---

11. MacDonald, George. "The Disciple," *The Disciple and Other Poems*, (Memphis: General Books, 2010), 21.

12. Rossetti, Christina. "Surely He hath borne our griefs," *The Complete Poems*, (New York: Penguin Books, 2001), 411.

13. I highly recommend *A Sacrifice of Praise*, Edited by James H. Trott, (Nashville: Cumberland, 1999).

"Shout for joy in the LORD, O you righteous! Praise befits the upright. Give thanks to the LORD with the lyre, make melody to him with the harp of ten strings! Sing to him a new song!" (Ps. 33:1-3). The Sons of Korah expressed their joy through music, saying, "My heart overflows with a pleasing theme; I address my verses to the king; my tongue is like the pen of a ready scribe" and inviting their listeners "Clap your hands, all peoples! Shout to God with loud songs of joy!" (Ps. 45:1, 47:1). Even the lament experienced by exiled Israelites is depicted in musical terms: "By the waters of Babylon, there we sat down and wept when we remembered Zion. On the willows there we hung up our lyres…How shall we sing the LORD's song in a foreign land?" (Ps. 137:1-2, 4).

In the book of Psalms, we find the whole spectrum of human emotion expressed to God through song. Placed at the center of the Scriptures, this collection of ancient songs shows the central role of music in the life of a believer. Our enjoyment of God through music need not be limited to spiritual songs, though the apostle Paul does remind us that they play a significant role of shaping our souls (Eph. 5:19). Madeline L'Engle wisely notes, "There is nothing so secular that it cannot be sacred, and that is one of the deepest messages of the Incarnation."[14] My teenagers and I have the most amazing conversations when I listen to their current playlists. We listen for the hunger for transcendence and hints of human longing. We discuss how Christ alone can satisfy the desires expressed through hip hop, R & B, and even pop. Listening to one another's favorite songs can serve as an avenue to get to know both strangers, friends, and family.

## Signals of Transcendence

While beauty provides a pathway for believers to worship their beautiful God, it is also a helpful way to introduce those outside the faith to our God. As we have already established, the arts

---

14. L'Engle, *Walking*, 42.

and nature are gifts of common grace, available to all people. While they are insufficient for salvation, they offer ramps into conversations which may lead to the presentation of the gospel. There is only one way to God, and that is through faith in Jesus Christ (John 14:6; Acts 4:12); however, there are many ways to come to know Christ. When people encounter transcendent beauty that stirs their souls, we have opportunities to engage them in conversations around the source of such beauty.

Peter Berger calls these moments "signals of transcendence" and defines them as "phenomena that are to be found within the domain of our 'natural' reality but that appear to point beyond that reality."[15] When someone is moved to tears by *Les Mis* or finds herself stirred by a concerto, these moments are flares that signal a hunger for more. As we learn to look and listen by cultivating our attention, we will find ourselves noticing the deeper longings of those around us (which is a form of attunement, a holy noticing). When we notice a signal of transcendence, we step towards our companions with empathetic curiosity, asking questions about their experiences and spiritual desires. With patience and attentiveness to the person before us and to the Spirit of God within us, we look for open doors for the Word of God to go forth (Col. 4:2-4). Like the apostle Paul, we ask for wisdom to know how to interact with outsiders, "making the best use of the time," letting our "speech be gracious, seasoned with salt," so that we might know how we ought to answer each person (Col. 4:5-6).

We can consider using (or adapting) some of the following questions to engage our friends spiritually through beauty:

- When is the last time that you were deeply moved by beauty?
- What longings or questions did that experience stir within you?

---

15. Berger, Peter. *A Rumor of Angels*, (Garden City: Doubleday, 1970), 53.

- Where do you think this beauty originates? How would you explain your transcendent experience?
- What if I told you that I know the source of that beauty? Would you be interested in hearing more about the God that created beauty?

## The Slowing of Sabbath

When I think about the potential pathways of beauty all around me, my first thought is "Yes!", but my second thought is "When?" After all, enjoying the beauty made available to us through nature and the arts requires both time and attention, two things that are hard to come by in our distracted and busy culture. Cultivating attention demands that we live at a different cadence than the dizzying world around us. Thankfully, our God has lovingly commanded such a pace through the Fourth Commandment to practice the Sabbath (Exod. 20:8-11; Deut. 5:12-15).

Our God is not a hard taskmaster like the pharaohs of Egypt or our current company bosses. He knows that we are limited beings and has created and modeled rhythms of rest for His children. Before sin or death entered the picture, God established the cadence of six days of work and one day of rest. In fact, the first thing God calls holy is time (Gen. 2:1-3). God, being unlimited and inexhaustible, did not rest because He was tired or weary from His world-making. He rested because rest is the proper complement for work. The first two chapters of Genesis feature a series of complementary pairs: light and dark, day and night, sky and sea, birds and fish, man and woman. Work and rest complete the series.[16]

On the other side of man's fall into sin, work became more wearisome, and the Sabbath became even more necessary. In our sin, we lose sight of who God is and who He says we are. We become human doings instead of human beings,

---

16. Peterson, Eugene. *Living the Resurrection: The Risen Christ in Everyday Life*, (Colorado Springs: Nav Press, 2006), 37.

striving and straining when we are already secure in Christ. The Sabbath serves as a weekly reminder to repent, rest, and remember as we recenter our lives around Christ who belongs on the throne of our hearts and at the center of our schedules.

As Abraham Heschel so powerfully writes, Sabbath reminds us that "The world has our hands, but our soul belongs to Someone Else."[17] Sabbath rest involves feasting on the Word and worshipping with God's people, but it is also an invitation to be re-created through things that we love and enjoy (which is at the heart of recreation). For one day a week, we are invited to set aside our striving so that we might be present to God and one another. Sabbath days offer opportunities to explore life-giving pathways like art, music, poetry, and nature. Sabbath rhythms slow us down so that we can see and savor our Savior and enjoy His manifold gifts towards us. Sabbath rest gets us off society's highways and allows us to explore the footpaths of beauty all around us.

Now that we have explored the pathway of beauty to cultivate attention in a distracting world, we will turn our attention to the pathway of pain. While this may seem like a hard cut, beauty and brokenness dwell together in our world: to be human is to know both. In a book about cultivating attention, I would be remiss if we did not honestly address the pathway of suffering as a means to cultivate our attention on Christ.

---

17. Heschel, Abraham Joshua. *The Sabbath,* (New York: Noonday Press, 1951), 13.

# Chapter Seven

# The Pathway of Pain

About once a month, I have a strange ritual I practice with the Lord. I walk into the local antique store and purchase between two and three beautiful, handstitched handkerchiefs. I take my time picking them and proudly tuck them into my purse to bring them home to store them in my desk drawer. They remain there until I get news of a suffering loved one. Then, I write a handwritten note and send one along to encourage the hurting to remember that we can hold two things at once. Beauty and brokenness are not mutually exclusive experiences, at least not before the second coming of Christ. The beautiful, dainty stitching is meant to remind the sufferer to keep their tear-swollen eyes open for beauty even amid the impossibly hard; the handkerchief itself is meant to dry their real tears and remind them of the day when God shall wipe every tear from every eye (Isa. 25:8, Rev. 21:4). In the handwritten note, I include the following short snippet from George Herbert's poem "The Dawning":

> "Arise, arise;
> And with his burial linen dry thine eyes:
> Christ left his graveclothes, that we might, when grief
> Draws tears, or blood, not want an handkerchief."[1]

---

1. Herbert, George. "The Dawning," *The Country Parson, The Temple*, (New York: Paulist Press, 1981), 233.

You see, suffering is a certainty for every human. Try as we may to avoid it, suffering interrupts our lives. Work as we do to prepare for it or insulate our lives against it with insurance policies and contingencies plans, suffering sobers, shocks, and surprises us still. Shock at suffering, even though we worship the Christ who suffered, is not an uncommon experience even for believers. The apostle Peter addressed it in the early church when believers were beginning to experience terrible persecution for their faith: "Beloved, do not be surprised at the fiery trial when it comes upon you to test you, as though something strange were happening to you. But rejoice insofar as you share Christ's sufferings, that you may also rejoice and be glad when his glory is revealed" (1 Pet. 4:12-13).

A few words stick out in Peter's handling of hardship among those whom he loved: *beloved*, *when*, and *rejoice*. When we suffer, our flesh sometimes responds by doubting God's love for us. We wonder, if God really loved us, why would He allow this to happen? Peter cuts through the doubts and reminds God's people that they are His beloved and chosen children, purchased by the precious blood of the Son (1 Pet. 1:17-19, 2:9). Their being *beloved* does not insulate them from suffering, for Peter uses the word *when* not *if*. Christ told His disciples the same thing to prepare their hearts for the suffering that was sure to come: "In this world you will have tribulation. But take heart, I have overcome the world" (John 16:33). Finally, Peter bids believers *rejoice* even as they experience the brokenness of this world. Peter's commandment to *rejoice* was not a glib statement. Remember, Peter saw his Savior suffer, but he also spent time with Christ post-resurrection. Peter saw the worst the world can do; however, Peter also saw firsthand the God who can work all things into His pattern for good (Rom. 8:28).

As we begin to explore suffering as a potential pathway for cultivating our attention, I do not want to flatten one of the most layered, nuanced, and personal realities a human can experience. Suffering is neither neat nor one-size-fits-all. I don't want to speak easily about something we experience dreadfully. Yet, I want to address the unexpected invitations and opportunities that suffering presents us as the Scriptures do. I don't want to shy away from the sobering and shaping power of suffering.

Suffering breeds comparison, as we tend to judge our suffering by the suffering of others. I want to undercut such comparison by offering Elisabeth Elliot's simple yet spacious definition of suffering as "wanting what we don't have or having what we don't want."[2] All suffering is suffering, and all suffering matters to God. If we must compare suffering, let us compare it with the weight of glory that it is producing for us (2 Cor. 4:16-18).

## The Sobering Reality of Suffering

Suffering has a way of taking center stage and getting our full and undivided attention. Consider Job. When we are introduced to Job, we meet a man whose life is marked by fullness, spiritually, relationally, physically, and emotionally. His home was full of children, his estate was full of flocks, and his heart was full of freedom and connection to God. As the story progresses, we watch his fullness leak out, misfortune after misfortune, into utter emptiness. Yet, all the suffering serves to focus Job's attention on God. Yes, the suffering broke him, but the breaking opened Job to a new experience of God's fullness (Job 42:1-6).

As Job's life literally comes apart piece by piece, there are many things he does not know. He does not know why any of this is happening, though as the reader, we know that God has allowed this series of suffering as a stage for His glory and Job's ultimate good. He does not know where to find God in the middle of his myriad suffering. In his own words, he says, "Oh, that I knew where I might find him, that I might come even to his seat!...Behold, I go forward, but he is not there;

---

2. Elliot, Elisabeth. *Suffering is Never for Nothing.* (Nashville: B & H, 2019), 9.

and backward, but I do not perceive him; on the left hand when he is working, I do not behold him; he turns to the right hand, but I do not see him" (Job 23:3, 8-9). He does not know when or how his suffering will end (Job 19:1-2). Suffering stirs and unsettles our souls as few other experiences can; however, suffering can also be an agent to sharpen our attention upon God.

Amid all that Job does not know, Job does know a few significant truths which steer him through his experience of suffering. He knows that God is both sovereign and good (Job 1:21, 9:4). Even though he can't seem to find God, he is convinced that, if he could, God would plead his case. He says confidently, "I would know what he would answer me and understand what he would say to me. Would he contend with me in the greatness of his power? No, he would pay attention to me. There an upright man could argue with him, and I would be acquitted by my judge" (Job 23:5-7). He knows that he needs an arbiter who could mediate between God and him (Job 9:32-33). By faith, he longs for one who could understand both God and man and act as reconciler between both parties, laying a hand on both. Even though he can't see or understand what God is doing, Job is convinced that God sees him and has good purposes for him. He says, "But he knows the way that I take; when he has tried me, I shall come out as gold" and "For I know that my Redeemer lives, and at the last he will stand upon the earth" (Job 23:10, 19:25).

Thousands of years before the incarnate Christ stepped into the story of our suffering, Job longed for someone who could make sense of his suffering. He begged God for the mediator that we know as the person of Christ, one fully God yet fully man who understood both God and the human experience. We know what Job could barely dream! There is one who makes sense of our suffering and fully perceives our pain. Christ's first coming validated human suffering and dealt with sin, its ultimate source. In His second coming, He will fully and finally remove us from sin's presence and eradicate all suffering.

In between, we will suffer, but we will never suffer alone (Matt. 28:20). We will grieve, but as those who have a living hope (2 Cor. 4:8-10; 1 Thess. 4:13; 1 Pet. 1:3-5).

## The Suffering Savior

The suffering servant whom Isaiah prophesied about, we see clearly in the person of Jesus Christ. He envisioned the tender shoot growing out of Jesse's stump; we stand under the shade of the mighty tree (Isa. 53:2; Matt. 13:31-32). When we wrestle with the portions of pain and cups of calamity God allows in our lives, we know there was one who drank the cup of suffering alone (Matt. 20:22, 26:36-46).

The writers of the New Testament constantly reminded the early church how Christ transformed the human experience of suffering. Christ, Son though He was, learned obedience through suffering (Heb. 2:10-11). As adopted sons and daughters of God, we too can expect to learn obedience through suffering (1 Pet. 4:1). In Christ, we have a high priest who was tempted in every way, yet was without sin. After atoning for our sin, He sat down at the right hand of God where He presently pleads for us as one who empathizes with our weakness (Heb. 4:14-15, 7:25). In our suffering, we can fix our eyes on the one who suffered to the point of death on our behalf (Heb. 12:1-4). The Second Person of the Trinity becomes the focal point upon which saints can steady themselves in the dizziness of suffering. Suffering does not have the last word, Christ does. In the scarred hands of our Savior, suffering becomes a shaping tool.

## Suffering Shapes Us

You've likely heard the proverb, "The same heat that melts the butter hardens the steel." Suffering shapes us whether for ill or good. We all know people who have experienced the same trauma very differently. The death of a child ruins one marriage yet strengthens another. An experience of betrayal in the local church leaves one person hardened and far from Christ and the church but another clinging even more closely to both Him and His bride. We don't get to choose the crosses we are called to carry, but we have some say in the way in which we carry them. Suffering breaks us, but breaking can be a means of opening us. Suffering can isolate us or drive us more deeply into community and companionship.

Few things shape us the way suffering does. Crises can become crucibles that refine and redirect us; perhaps this is why trials in the Scriptures are often likened to refining fires. When Christ first began to drop hints of His coming suffering, Peter responded in the flesh, saying, "Far be it from you, Lord! This shall never happen to you!" (Matt. 16:22). Clearly, at this point in his spiritual maturation, Peter did not understand the shaping power of suffering. Jesus responds by teaching about the necessity of cross-carrying for His disciples: "If anyone would come after me, let him deny himself and take up his cross and follow me" (Matt. 16:24). Many years of maturation later, we find a very different Peter with a very different view on suffering in the life of the believer. Before being martyred on an upside down cross, Peter gently reminded the early church that suffering can serve as a refining fire: "In this you rejoice, though now for a little while, if necessary, you have been grieved by various trials, so that the tested genuineness of your faith—more precious than gold that perishes though it is tested by fire—may be found to result in praise and glory and honor at the revelation of Jesus Christ" (1 Pet. 1:6-7).

Our perspective on suffering can result in either stunted growth or increased growth. We have known about post-traumatic stress disorder (PTSD) and its accompanying neurological effects on the brain for quite some time; however, recently researchers have begun to study the potential for post-traumatic growth. Post-traumatic growth does not deny the lingering effects of suffering on the human mind and body; however, it does begin to show that suffering also provides shaping opportunities. As believers, we ought not to be surprised when science confirms what the Scriptures have always told us to be true: there are gifts that only suffering offers us. In times of suffering, we cling to the Word of God with the focused attention that comes from pain and desperation (Ps. 119:71). Our ears become deeply attuned to His Word, for we know that we have nowhere else to run but to the one who offers us eternal life (John 6:68). Our eyes look to Him and wait for Him more than watchmen for the morning or a maid with her lady (Pss. 130:6, 123:2).

## The Megaphone of Suffering

Suffering simultaneously silences the white noise all around us and augments our attention towards God. Have you ever noticed that in movies, when someone gets terrible news, the background noise usually goes silent? All the sounds of life are hushed as the person tries to make sense of the news. The directors are merely mirroring in externalities what happens when unexpected and unwelcome suffering enters our life.

Sitting in a sterile hospital room to hear about a biopsy, we suddenly don't hear the normal noise of nurses chatting and machines beeping. When our child calls to tell us they have been in a serious car accident, the sounds of normal life recede to the background. When we get an email informing us the company is downsizing, we no longer hear the office chatter or the sounds of people typing. Suffering silences the white noise; the silence creates space for our souls to hear from God. C. S. Lewis wisely noted, "God whispers to us in our pleasures, speaks in our conscience, but shouts in our pain: it is His megaphone to rouse a deaf world."[3]

Suffering quiets surface noise and focuses our attention on the needs of our souls. When we suffer, we don't settle for the cheap words of worldly comfort; we cling to the life-giving words of the Scripture. Nothing else will do. The psalmist said with confidence after a season of suffering, "Before I was

---

3. Lewis, C.S. *The Problem of Pain*, (San Francisco: Harper, 2001), 91.

afflicted, I went astray, but now I keep your word" (Ps. 119:67). Moses' long suffering as the leader of God's wayward people made him long for God's Word and His presence: "Return, O LORD! How long? Have pity on your servants! Satisfy us in the morning with your steadfast love, that we may rejoice and be glad all our days. Make us glad for as many days as you have afflicted us, and for as many years as we have seen evil" (Ps. 90:13-15). David's experiences of suffering helped him hunger for the Lord's nearness and help: "With my voice, I cry out to the LORD; with my voice, I plead for mercy to the LORD. I pour out my complaint before him; I tell my trouble before him" (Ps. 142:1-2).

While the psalmists, Moses, and David were longing for the Word of God to come to them through a prophet, we have Christ, the better prophet. God has spoken to us finally and most fully through the person and work of Jesus Christ. The writer of Hebrews assures the Jewish believers, "Long ago, at many times and in many ways, God spoke to our fathers by the prophets, but in these last days he has spoken to us by his Son" (Heb. 1:1-2). When we suffer, like Job, we rightly ask questions: *Why is this happening? How will I endure? When will this end?* God, being a good and attentive Father welcomes our questions and quiets us with His love. However, it is helpful to remember something Watchman Nee said many years ago: "It will help us greatly and save us from much confusion, if we keep constantly before us this fact, that God will answer all our questions in one way and one way only, namely, by showing us more of His Son."[4]

## Suffering Sharpens Sight

It seems strange to say that suffering can focus our attention when it seems to blur both our minds and senses. Suffering and grief make our brains feel fuzzy, forgetful, and fatigued.

---

4. Nee, Watchman. *The Normal Christian Life*, (Carol Stream: Tyndale, 1977), 12.

In seasons of intense suffering, we forget to do normal things like eating, drinking water, and showering. But suffering can also sharpen our senses even as it seems to blur our minds.

I remember reading a book written by a Vietnam veteran who wrote honestly not only about the horrors he saw in Vietnam, but also about his experiences of color and beauty in Vietnam. It wasn't that the colors changed or were brighter there; it was more that living on the thin edge between life and death made him see more clearly both the beauty and brokenness of earth. Corrie ten Boom, while living in the nightmare that was a concentration camp, remembers moments of being utterly stunned by the beauty of a bird or a small flower or blade of grass. She recalls the following instance of sharpened sight:

> I looked down and saw some blades of grass and some shepherd's purse growing between the paving stones. When the guard was not looking I quickly bent down, picked a handful, and put them inside my dress. After the interrogation was over, when I was back in my cell, I found an old broken medicine bottle and arranged my flowers in it...It was my garden, the only beautiful thing in my cell.[5]

If you want to be re-enchanted with the everyday things we take for granted, spend time with someone who is suffering. The wonders of a delicious meal, the comfort of a strong embrace, and the sound of songbirds chirping outside are not lost on them as they are on us.

One of the most memorable books I read in the past few years recounted a woman's enjoyment of a snail as she convalesced in her room from a severe neurological condition. I know it sounds strange but hear her out. The once active writer, in what was supposed to be the prime of her life, found herself bound to bed. She recounts, "As the months drifted by,

---

5. Rosewell, Pamela. *The Five Silent Years of Corrie Ten Boom*, (Grand Rapids: Zondervan, 1986), 63.

it was hard to remember why the endless details of a healthy life and a good job seemed so critical. It was odd to see my friends overwhelmed by their busy lives, when they could do all the things I could not, without a second thought."[6] Stilled by suffering, she found comfort, beauty, and wonder through her surprising encounters with a snail. She began to realize the power of attention in the middle of her affliction. She muses, "Survival often depends on a specific focus: a relationship, a belief, or a hope balanced on the edge of possibility,"[7] and she found surprising consolation through the contours of a snail. With her attention freed from all the demands of the busy world, she discovered the depth of wonder found in focusing it on something as mundane as a mollusk.

As believers in Christ, we have a far better focal point: we get to focus our attention on the creator of every creature, the God of the universe who became man that we might hope in eternal life with Him. Suffering trains our eyes not only to see sharply but also to see through. Suffering cuts through the gauze of this earth and removes its shiny veneer. It exposes much of the laughter of earth as hollow and many of its pleasures as transitory. Suffering can serve as a powerful spotlight to show us what matters most in life. When a loved one is in hospice, we don't care about the upcoming bills or the emails stacking up in our inbox. Suffering reshuffles our lives and forces us to reprioritize considering eternity.

When suffering seems to tarry, we say with the psalmist, "My soul longs for your salvation; I hope in your word. My eyes long for your promise; I ask, When will you comfort me?" (Ps. 119:81-82). When life on earth here below seems to be coming apart, we lift our eyes above to the life-giver (Ps.121). When suffering makes our lives on earth feel unbearable, we say with the apostle, "But according to his promise we are

---

6. Bailey, Elisabeth Tova. *The Sound of a Wild Snail Eating*, (Chapel Hill: Algonquin Books, 2010), 11.

7. Ibid, 15.

waiting for new heavens and a new earth in which righteousness dwells" (2 Pet. 3:13). When our afflictions seem too heavy to bear, we fix our gaze on the coming weight of glory which far surpasses even the heftiest burdens (2 Cor. 4:16-18).

## Suffering Exposes Us

To add insult to injury, when we experience suffering, our hearts are exposed. As if the external havoc seasons of suffering wreak were not enough, suffering also reveals our inner lives. Initially, pain and trials act like an interrogator's search light, uncovering our inordinate loves, our entitlement, our false dependence on the things of earth, our transactional ways of interacting with God, and our impatience. We don't realize how much hope we have in the things of the earth until they are taken away from us. We don't notice the unspoken formulas we have placed upon God until it seems like He is not upholding His end of our one-sided bargains. We think we are building our houses upon the rock until the storm reveals all the sand upon which we are attempting to stand (Matt. 7:24-27).

It helps me to remember that God only exposes us to clothe us with His righteousness. When He disciplines us, it is always for our good and His glory. When He reveals the sin-sickness in our hearts, it is only to lead us swiftly to our great and gentle physician (Matt. 9:12). When we realize that our Savior is the wounded healer, instead of resisting the search, we begin to pray with David, "Search me, O God, and know my heart! Try me and know my thoughts! And see if there be any grievous way in me, and lead me in the way everlasting" (Ps. 139:23-24). Rather than running from the scalpel that is the Word of the God, we run to God and lay ourselves under His Word (Heb. 4:12-13).

In his poem "East Coker," T.S. Eliot captures the beauty of being in the hands of the Wounded Healer.

> The wounded surgeon plies the steel
> That questions the distempered part;

> Beneath the bleeding hands we feel
> The sharp compassion of the healer's art
> Resolving the enigma of the fever chart...
>
> The whole earth is our hospital,
> Endowed by the ruined millionaire,
> Wherein, if we do well, we shall
> Die of the absolute paternal care
> That will not leave us, but prevents us everywhere.[8]

Our God loves us enough to offer us what Eliot aptly calls his "sharp compassion." All the suffering we experience passes through His scarred hands and is allowed and steered by His heart which is full of kind intentions towards His children (Eph. 3:1-6). There will be many moments when we don't understand His hands, but we must always trust His heart. As Paul reminded the Church in Rome, "He who did not spare his own Son but gave him up for us all, how will he not also with him graciously give us all things?" (Rom. 8:32).

As soon as suffering exposes us, our Savior stands ready to clothe us in His robes of righteousness. As suffering shines its searchlight on us, we can choose to focus the beam of our attention away from our sin and towards our Savior who dealt with it once and for all (Heb. 10:12-14).

## The Sixth Sense of Suffering

Suffering not only sharpens our senses, both physically and spiritually, but also provides a potential sixth sense. The uncomfortable stretching suffering causes can serve to strengthen our capacity for empathy. Those who have suffered or are presently suffering can be more attuned to the silent suffering of others. When life is full and our senses are preoccupied, we tend to fly past the fractured and the frail.

---

8. Eliot, T.S. "East Coker," *The Complete Poems and Plays,* (Boston: Faber and Faber, 1969), 181.

Suffering slows our pace and opens our eyes to the needs of others around us. Suffering offers us deeper sight of the people around us.

Jesus, whose sinless heart was never hardened, saw and sensed the pain of those around Him, even in crowds. Once, when Jesus was leaving Jericho, a well-known beggar named Bartimaeus continually cried out, "Son of David, have mercy on me!" (Mark 10:46-48). The crowds rebuked him, urging him to be quiet, but Jesus brought him near and restored his sight (Mark 10:49-52). In another crowd, while rushing to heal the beloved daughter of Jairus, Jesus stopped to care for a less-doted-upon daughter. She merely hoped to touch the hem of His garment for healing, but Jesus went well beyond her physical healing. Sensing her shame and isolation, He noticed her and named her "daughter" (Mark 5:21-34). Even on the cross as He was suffering unthinkable agony, Jesus sensed the needs of those around Him. Jesus assured the thief on the cross of His forgiveness, offering spiritual and relational balm (Luke 23:43).

Those who have suffered have been taken to deeper depths than they likely would have chosen for themselves; however, they also have mined the treasures of the darkness (Isa. 45:3). They understand from experience that a man's heart is deep waters, but a man of understanding can draw him or her out (Prov. 20:5). They step toward a hurting world with the comfort with which they have been comforted (2 Cor. 1:3-6). They are unlikely to offer simple solutions to complex problems and more willing to sit in the complexity and point us to Christ.

I love the proverb of Amy Carmichael: "If souls can suffer alongside, and I hardly know it, because the spirit of discernment is not in me, then I know nothing of Calvary love."[9] One of the hidden gifts of suffering is a tender-heartedness to the sufferings of others.

---

9. Carmichael, Amy. *If,* (Fort Washington: Christian Literature Crusade, 1938), 56.

## Learning to Lament

Christians are not called to a life of stoicism and to a stiff upper lip amid suffering. The same God who braided us together body, mind and soul invites us to bring all of ourselves into His presence. In Chapter Four, we touched briefly on lament as a means to pay attention to God even in the middle of our pain; however, it is fitting in this chapter to spend some time revisiting God's good gift of lament. Mark Vroegop, who learned about lament by living it, wrote the following about this gift of the darkness: "You may think lament is the opposite of praise. It isn't. Instead, lament is a path to praise as we are led through our brokenness and disappointment."[10]

God invites us to bring ourselves authentically into His presence, which means we need to start by being honest with ourselves. David bids us, "Trust in him at all times, O people; pour out your heart before him; God is a refuge for us" (Ps. 62:8). We cannot bring into God's presence what we refuse to note or name. As C.S. Lewis noted in a letter to a friend about earnestness in prayer, "We must lay before Him what is in us, not what ought to be in us."[11] In lament, we learn to pay appropriate attention to what is happening within us so that we can bring it into the light of God's presence. Though the attention begins within, it moves upward and outward as we learn to lament.

Lamentations, an entire book of lament in the Scriptures, offers modern souls a primer on the art of paying attention to our grief and pouring our hearts out to the Lord. In it, we come alongside Jeremiah, "the weeping prophet," as he honestly processes his raw emotions with God. Jeremiah's attention gradually shifts from his anguish to the character of his God:

---

10. Vroegop, Mark. *Dark Clouds, Deep Mercy*, (Wheaton: Crossway, 2019), 28.
11. Lewis, C.S. *Letters to Malcolm* (London: William Collins, 2020), 27.

Remember my affliction and my wanderings, the wormwood and the gall! My soul continually remembers it and is bowed down within me. But this I call to mind and therefore I have hope: The steadfast love of the LORD never ceases; his mercies never come to an end; they are new every morning; great is your faithfulness. 'The LORD is my portion,' says my soul, 'therefore I will hope in him. (Lam. 3:19-24)

## Suffering as Limited Time Offer

In our advertisement-heavy culture, we are all-too familiar with the phrase "Limited Time Offer." It is intended to induce urgency and propel us into action. I want to borrow a phrase from the world and bathe it in the truths of Scripture, because, as strange as it sounds, suffering is a limited time offer. For the believer, suffering is punctuated (it will end), purposed (it is never wasted), and productive (it accomplishes God's will and works for our good). Our short time on this earth is our only chance to suffer redemptively with Jesus (Col. 1:24-25). Our numbered days here are our only chance to know the comfort of the Holy Spirit, for comfort assumes discomfort (John 14:26). Only on earth can we offer our eyes to cry empathetic tears with and for the sorrowing, for there will be no more crying in the presence of Christ. Suffering can serve to focus our attention on God. Those are limited time offers I don't want us to miss. It may not be the deal you were looking for, but it is one that Christ knows you need.

# Conclusion

We've come a long way together, you and me. We began our journey together by taking a long, loving look at our attentive God. Then, we learned about the connection between our attention and our affection. We took a long, hard look at our sin that leads to distraction, and then took a relieving look back at our Savior. We learned about the power of faith focused on the person and work of Jesus Christ. We explored different forms of creativity and traveled down the pathways of presence, beauty, and even pain. I am so thankful for the extended attention you have expended in reading thus far. In a culture marked by decreasing attention spans, you've invested your time and attention to read a book about cultivating attention. Such a sacrifice is not lost on me. What likely began as diversive curiosity you have channeled into epistemic curiosity, and I hope you are richer for such a costly investment.

It has been my perpetual prayer that those who read this book would have their gaze focused on the person of Christ long enough to be transformed. My words are inert, but His words are our very life (Deut. 32:47). My prayer is that this book would merely be the beginning of the lifelong process of learning to pay attention to your inattention. As we learned, attention cultivates affection, and affection compels conduct. If our end goal is to be like Christ and near Christ, we need to cultivate habits of faith-filled concentration upon Him.

The dizzying, distracting world waits for you, but so does the God who is infinitely worth waiting upon! More importantly, there are people who have never known an attentive gaze of love who wait to be loved with God's everlasting, agape love. As much as I want us to offer them the beams of our attention, I want more for us to sit longer and more often under the beam of His agape affection.

The more we see Him, the more we will speak of Him (Acts 4:20). The more we sit in His presence, the more we will become present people. One day, we will fix our gaze fully on Him, but in the meanwhile, we make it our aim to practice repenting and returning to His long and loving gaze (1 Cor. 13:12; 1 John 3:2-3).

Also available from Christian Focus ...

# Intentional Interruptions

LEARNING TO BE INTERRUPTED THE WAY GOD INTENDED

JONATHAN THOMAS

# Intentional Interruptions

## Learning to Be Interrupted the Way God Intended

Jonathan Thomas

We are busy and constantly bombarded. Notifications, pings, alerts: we carry in our pockets devices that are designed to capture and keep our attention. We are never fully present, always thinking ahead to the next thing, distracted by an email, playing worries over in our minds. But what effect is this having on our lives, relationships and, most importantly, our spiritual health?

We need rest – the rest that only Christ can give. But this book is not simply meant to get you off your phone, make more time to stop, or help you simplify and digitally detox. Instead, you are invited into the greatest life imaginable, where we have the openness to be interrupted by God and used in a way that will bring Him glory.

At the end of each chapter, Thomas encourages us to take time to ponder and pray – or Selah – and gives us guiding questions to consider. A challenging read for anyone who feels overwhelmed by all that calls on their attention and for those who long for peace.

# Deep Simplicity

## MEDITATIONS ON
## ABIDING IN CHRIST

---

EMILY DARNELL

# Deep Simplicity

## Meditations on Abiding in Christ

### Emily Darnell

To abide is to remain, to rest, to dwell, to be at home. Emily Darnell encourages readers to truly abide in God and His Word, not just to read a couple of verses, but to take time to meditate on it and be nourished. Each chapter will unfold an aspect of abiding, ending with some practices to incorporate in personal worship, or Scriptures to meditate upon to grow deeper in grace, and in knowledge and love of the One who loved you first.

---

One of the most wonderful promises Christ has given us is to be with us always, but what does it mean to practise His presence and enjoy His transforming friendship? Here is a remarkable book of meditations on one of the most vital but most neglected aspects of Christian living. Every page is rich in biblical wisdom to be savoured phrase by phrase. If you read slowly and reflect prayerfully, this sharply focused book will deepen your devotion to Christ, nurture your inner life, and align your thoughts with eternity.

Jonathan Lamb
Minister–at–large for Keswick Ministries

# Christian Focus Publications

Our mission statement –

STAYING FAITHFUL

In dependence upon God we seek to impact the world through literature faithful to His infallible Word, the Bible. Our aim is to ensure that the Lord Jesus Christ is presented as the only hope to obtain forgiveness of sin, live a useful life and look forward to heaven with Him.

Our books are published in four imprints:

## CHRISTIAN FOCUS

Popular works including biographies, commentaries, basic doctrine and Christian living.

## CHRISTIAN HERITAGE

Books representing some of the best material from the rich heritage of the church.

## MENTOR

Books written at a level suitable for Bible College and seminary students, pastors, and other serious readers. The imprint includes commentaries, doctrinal studies, examination of current issues and church history.

## CF4·K

Children's books for quality Bible teaching and for all age groups: Sunday school curriculum, puzzle and activity books; personal and family devotional titles, biographies and inspirational stories – because you are never too young to know Jesus!

Christian Focus Publications Ltd,
Geanies House, Fearn, Ross-shire,
IV20 1TW, Scotland, United Kingdom.
www.christianfocus.com